The organization of gold mining business with specimens of the departmental books and the account books

Nicol Brown

THE ORGANIZATION

OF

GOLD MINING BUSINESS,

WITH SPECIMENS OF THE

DEPARTMENTAL REPORT BOOKS

AND THE

ACCOUNT BOOKS.

BY

NICOL BROWN.

SECOND EDITION.

"*Nulla dies sine linea.*"

GLASGOW:

DUNCAN CAMPBELL & SON, 96 ST. VINCENT STREET.

LONDON: E. & F. N. SPON, LIMITED, 125 STRAND.

NEW YORK: {SPON & CHAMBERLAIN, 123 LIBERTY STREET
ENGINEERING AND MINING JOURNAL, 161 BROADWAY.

CAPE TOWN, PORT ELIZABETH, AND JOHANNESBURG, J. C. JUTA & CO.

1903.

GENERAL

ERRATA

On page 39, line 26, for "page 181," read "page 179"

,, 54, lines 1 and 2, for "Expenditure Sheet (No 8), page 149," read "Wages Summary, page 149, Stores Summary, page 157, and Expenditure Sheet (No 8), page 163"

,, 61, lines 34 and 35, for "Expenditure Sheet (No 8), page 149," read "Wages Summary page 149, Stores Summary, page 157 and Expenditure Sheet (No 8) page 163"

,, 85, lines 21 and 22, for "Expenditure Sheet (No 8), page 149," read "Wages Summary page 149, Stores Summary, page 157, and Expenditure Sheet (No 8) page 163"

, 106 line 5, for "page 170," read "page 163"

, 106, ,, 16, ,, ,, ,, ,,

,, 106, ,, 19, "Sundries" "Erection of New Plant Account

,, 113, ,, 15, ,, "duplicate," ,, "corresponding"

,, 134, under "Note," delete "(Form 8)"

 136, under upper "Note," delete "(Form 8)"

PRINTED AT THE MYRTLE PRESS GLASGOW,
BY DUNCAN CAMPBELL & SON

TABLE OF CONTENTS.

NOTE.

THE "DEPARTMENTAL REPORT BOOKS" required may be suitably made of the same size of paper as the Specimens shewn in the following pages.

The "ACCOUNT BOOKS" should be larger in size than the Specimens, preferably of what is known as demy paper.

The copies of the Departmental Reports and Accounts, for transmission monthly to the Head Office, see page 207 should be on the same Form and size of paper as the originals.

This Book should always be in duplicate—one copy at the Mine and one at the Head Office of the Company—for reference purposes.

Any local variations which are authorized by the Head Office should be noted in both the Books. Convenient spaces have been left for this purpose, and for other MS. notes.

PREFACE TO FIRST EDITION.

THE system of organization presented in this book is the outcome of a large and varied experience acquired by the compiler in connection with numerous Mining and Metallurgical Works from the year 1869 to the present time.

When the compiler first began to deal with the subject in hand, there was no written authority on the subject, nor any standard Forms suitable for Mining Accounts; nor were the methods set forth in this book at all familiar in mining circles. Forms were gathered, verbally and otherwise, from older and more experienced men; but it was found that those who had some claim to be authorities on the subject were far from being in agreement in their methods, while professional accountants, otherwise, no doubt, skilled enough in their general business, but with no knowledge of the distinctive character of the system of accounts required for mining, only made matters more perplexing by initiating systems of accounts which, to practical mining men, were useless, or it might be misleading.

During the long course of years above referred to, it has been the duty of the compiler to formulate sets of rules similar to the present, and these have been printed privately and issued to friends only; but the fact that these were coming into use outside of the compiler's own circle, led him recently to publish a limited edition of "Specimens of Working Records and Account Books designed for Gold Mining Companies," which is now, in a revised and more complete form, submitted under a new title.

The main object aimed at is to harmonize the records of the working or technical and of the business or commercial departments, so that the responsible officers may understand and follow the results recorded by each other, and that the whole system of departmental reports and accounts may be so fitted in and dovetailed together as to be rendered intelligible to a London Board.

Another object, of scarcely less importance, is to secure uniformity in the classification and tabulation of the results and operations of different companies, so that they may be readily and accurately compared and contrasted.

The general purport and objects of the whole work may be briefly summarized as follows :—

I. That a well-considered design and purpose should run through the whole business arrangements, that the work of the commercial and technical departments should be reconciled and co-ordinated, and every man know his place and his work.

II. That the information received from the Mines should be of the fullest possible character. The Returns to the Head Office should therefore be complete copies of the originals in the Mines books.

III. That the entire expenditure should be restricted to certain well-defined accounts, which, in the specimens given, are as follows :—Wages, Stores Issued, General Charges, and Sundries—leaving the departmental allocations to be set out in the schedule provided, and thereby dispensing entirely, if possible, with transfer entries and the splitting up of items of expenditure. The system of keeping numerous DEPARTMENTAL LEDGER ACCOUNTS, to which the wages and stores are constantly being distributed, is a cumbersome one.

IV. That uniformity in definition and classification should be observed, so that comparison of the operations and results of different Companies may be facilitated for economic and other purposes (see page 163).

V. That the Accounts should be so kept that the cost of the work done and the rate per ton, foot, or other unit, may be clearly tabulated and shewn at every step under its proper head or sub-head of expenditure.

VI. That everything done at the works should be so recorded that, if required, a periodical inspection, by competent Engineers and Accountants, may be facilitated.

VII. That facility of reference to every part should be secured.

Although, for the sake of clearness, it has been found advisable to illustrate the Forms by concrete examples, it is not intended to advocate any particular process or method as regards technical matters, or even any special system of book-keeping, so long as the necessary results are shewn in a convenient form: the manner of recording the results rather than the means of arriving at them, is the object here in view.

As regards technical matters, the choice of methods must always remain with the engineering and other technical advisers of the Company.

To ensure that the Forms dealing with technical matters should be as complete as possible, the compiler has availed himself of the assistance of the gentlemen mentioned below.

The following parts have been drafted or revised by MR. R. G. ELWES, M.Inst. C.E. :—

Report Book **A,** Surface Prospecting.
      ,,   **B,** Underground Prospecting.
      ,,   **C,** Mining and Ore Transport.

MR. ELWES has also drawn the Notes on Plans on page 25 and the short article on Mines Redemption (on page 127)—a subject often too much neglected by Mining Companies.

The following have been drafted or revised by MR. M. T. BROWN, B.Sc. A.M.Inst.C.E. :—

Report Book **D,**   Milling and Crushing.
      ,,   **Fa,** Power—Steam.
      ,,   **Fc,** Oil Engines.
      ,,   **G,**   Maintenance of Plant.

The Cyaniding Report Book **E** has been revised by MR. J. S. MACARTHUR, F.C.S.
The Electrical Report Book **Fb,** has been revised by MR. JOHN RENNIE, M.Inst.E.E.

With regard to the Book-keeping System, many valuable suggestions have been received from MR. WILLIAM NEIL, Chartered Accountant, and have been embodied herein.

Many of the officers of different Mining Companies with which the compiler has been connected over a long period of years, have also rendered him valuable assistance by their suggestions.

The set of Forms contained in this book is intended to provide for the recording of all such operations and routine work as are usual in the ordinary run of Gold Mining Companies. To include every possible modification would have been cumbersome, and some are included which may not be required by many Companies. Upon the general principle here indicated, however, it would be easy to design special forms for particular requirements—such, for example, as Hydraulicing or Dredging river beds for Gold, and the new processes for Slime treatment. The main point to be kept in view is, that the responsible Engineers should, at the outset, divide off the several operations upon a systematic plan, such as described, to be submitted to their Boards for approval.

The system of Accounts here set forth is intended for the working records of the Company, and not of course, for publication in detail: but from these data the condensed Accounts to be presented to Shareholders can easily be prepared.

The plan adopted by Railway Companies of annexing to their Accounts a certificate that the Buildings, Plant, Machinery, &c., are in an efficient state of repair, should be followed by Mining Companies also, with the addition of a clause that the amount written off for depreciation is reasonable and sufficient. A specimen of such a certificate is given on page 129.

To the management of many mines already well organised this book may not present many features of novelty; but where no systematic directions have been formulated, it may still be profitable that they should be made, and it is hoped that hints for that purpose may be found in this book.

The compiler would ask the attention of Directors and Members of Chambers of Mines to the question of the proper demarcation of the Divisions under which the Expenditure in the Working Accounts is grouped (see page 163). On this and any other point he invites suggestions, for a future edition.

SUFFOLK HOUSE, CANNON STREET,
LONDON, E.C., 22nd June, 1897.

PREFACE TO SECOND EDITION.

IN issuing a second edition of this work, the Compiler acknowledges the kind reception the first edition has had, particularly in America.

The edition now issued has been brought up to date as much as possible, and several new forms have been added.

Amongst others a form for Slimes Treatment has been added, and alternate forms given for Mining and Ore Transport, and for Cyaniding Sands.

The Gold statement has been remodelled and based on the results of Wet Crushing, instead of Dry Crushing, as in the former edition.

The principles on which "Ore in Sight" should be estimated, as recommended by the Institution of Mining and Metallurgy, London, are set forth, as they cannot be made known too widely.

The chapter entitled "Profit and Loss, Ancient and Modern," has been introduced. It is a revised and extended edition of a paper read before the Glasgow Philosophical Society in 1894, and is suggestive of the direct points at issue to make profits in this business.

The chapter following indicates how the system at the Head Office should be arranged so as to be in harmony with the system at the Mines, as set out in detail herein.

The manner of obtaining facts at the Mine are minutely shewn in this book. The work of the Head Office is to scan and make use of the facts so obtained, so that the business may be properly understood and controlled, and hence this chapter.

If any Company wishes to begin a new system of statistics for its Mines, then the organization in the following pages is recommended as fairly complete, and elastic enough to be varied to suit local conditions; on the other hand, it is to be remembered that it is often a mistake to disturb settled systems, although not so complete as they might be. It is, however, possible to introduce improvements into settled systems, little by little, and the pages herein may assist in doing so. Good systems usually fit into each other's parts if well devised.

As referred to in other words in the former preface, there is nothing in these pages which professes to bring order and method to those who possess them, but only to those who have them not

Many of the forms and accounts are suitable for the use of Mining Companies other than gold.

The Compiler acknowledges the great help he has received from many friends, both scientific and literary, who have assisted him in a variety of ways, particularly in the chapter titled " The Profit and Loss of Gold Mining Ancient and Modern "

SUFFOLK HOUSE, CANNON STREET,
LONDON, E C., *28th September, 1903*

THE STAFF ARRANGEMENTS.

Introduction.

THE scientific and practical attainments required for the efficient working of a Gold Mine are now so numerous that it would be unreasonable to expect the General Manager of a Mine to be an expert in all the branches himself. He should, however, have the necessary skilled assistance in every department; and in order that ample provision may be made for the proper distribution of the Assistants' work the directions in the following pages have been drawn up.

The absence of such directions leads to friction and disorder.

In small Mines it may be impossible to have as many heads of departments as are herein provided; two or more departments may often have one head, the Records, however, still being kept separate. As an instance of combined duties, the Commercial Superintendent may act as Accountant; the Metallurgist may also act as Assayer, or the Underground Prospecting Report and the Mining and Ore Transport Report Books may be in charge of one official; other similar combinations may be formed, depending on the amount of work to be done in each department, and on the fitness of individual officers to undertake work not falling strictly in their own special field.

The Commercial Superintendent is placed in such a position of authority that the burden of many business arrangements may be taken off the General Manager's hands.

It will be observed, in reference to the divisions dealing with the Working Reports, that the responsible officer in charge is himself required to write up the Working Reports or Log Books. This, however, does not apply to the books which are referred to under the head of the Commercial Superintendent, and for which he is the responsible officer, the clerical work of which may be done by junior clerks.

The diagram given on page 40 shews the distribution of the work under the headings of the principal departments.

THE GENERAL MANAGER.

The General Manager should be a thoroughly trained Mining Engineer, and he should have control of the whole of the staff.

This book does not profess in any way to teach either Mining or Metallurgy; but it does profess to shew how the expenditure of cash in the different parts of the mining and metallurgical processes, now in general use, may be followed in detail, and recorded in such a way as to be intelligible to the Directors and the Shareholders who provide the money for carrying on the business. Long delays, sometimes extending over years, are incident to all kinds of mining operations; meanwhile, those who supply the capital are naturally anxious, and have the right, to know how it is being spent. If the methods of reporting progress and expenditure are left to the discretion of Managers, uniformity of system between different Mines cannot be expected, hence the advantage of a system which can be applied to every case is obvious.

Such a system will enable a Manager of a practical type, who has not been familiar with the details of office arrangements, to follow and control these.

Those duties of the General Manager and Commercial Superintendent, which are of a joint character, are defined on the next page.

THE COMMERCIAL SUPERINTENDENT.

This officer is to assist the General Manager with the commercial or business part of the work. He is next in authority after the General Manager, and in the latter's absence, usually acts for him, unless otherwise arranged by the Board of Directors. With regard to the following matters, the duties of the General Manager and the Commercial Superintendent are properly of a joint character; and in the case of requisitions and orders for Cash and Stores, and the signing of cheques (see page 91), the Board must initiate the method of procedure in each case :—

REQUISITIONS FOR CASH TO BE SUPPLIED BY THE HEAD OFFICE.
REQUISITIONS FOR STORES TO BE SUPPLIED BY THE HEAD OFFICE.
ORDERS GIVEN FOR STORES TO LOCAL MERCHANTS.
CORRESPONDENCE.
REGISTER OF LETTERS RECEIVED.
REGISTER OF PLANS.
REGISTER OF SAMPLES RECEIVED TO BE ASSAYED.
REGISTER OF ASSAY RESULTS.

It may be generally noted that all the operations, as shewn on the DEPARTMENTAL FORMS **A** to **G**, are under the direct control of the General Manager, who is the responsible head of the whole undertaking.

The STORES AND CASH ACCOUNT BOOKS (Nos. **1** to **8**) and the GOLD STATEMENT (No. **9**) are under the control of the Commercial Superintendent, and are to be kept on the lines laid down in the specimens.

The GENERAL EXPENDITURE SHEET (No. **8**) gathers up into one statement the summary of the total expenditure for the month, with the necessary references to the Forms **A** to **G** for the details of the work done, thus affording a complete evidence of how the money has been spent in each of the separate departments indicated by the letters.

The GOLD STATEMENT (No. **9**) also collects in one sheet the particulars of the Auriferous Ore treated, as given on Forms **C, D, E.** The amount of Gold Contents in the Ore treated, the amount of Gold extracted therefrom by the process, and the amount lost in process, as certified by the Assays made at the various stages of the process, are all brought together in one Statement and clearly reconciled and agreed.

THE ASSAYER.

The duties of this officer are to assay the ore, tailings, residues, and bullion, thereby enabling the General Manager to control and check the efficiency of the operations going on at every stage in the Mines and Metallurgical Works.

The checking of the gold contents of ore in all its stages is of vital importance to a business of this kind; and the whole value of the Departmental Reports and figures may be rendered worthless and misleading if the assaying be not done with scientific exactness.

The want of a proper system of taking samples has brought assays into unmerited disrepute with mining men,—the fact usually being that the sample only is at fault from not being truly representative of the bulk of the ore sampled.

It is of importance, therefore, that the sampling, which precedes the assaying, should receive great attention. Specimen methods of sampling are to be found on pages 29 to 35.

An assay plan of the Mine is of great assistance to the Manager, and should be prepared wherever possible.

SPACE RESERVED FOR MS. NOTES.

THE STAFF

The staff appointments should be nearly all made by the Board, and the engagements as made advised to the General Manager   It is recommended that those marked by an asterisk should be so appointed

I   The special work of the following has already been referred to —

> * **GENERAL MANAGER.**
> * **COMMERCIAL SUPERINTENDENT**
> * **ASSAYER.**

II   The other officers *arranged according to the sequence of the work or process*, are as follows the evidence of their work being recorded in the subsequent special Forms lettered **A** to **G** —

> **A** **SURFACE PROSPECTOR.**
> * **B** **MINE SURVEYOR. MINE FOREMAN OR CAPTAIN**
> * **C** **MINING ENGINEER OR MINE SURVEYOR.**
> **D** **MILL SUPERINTENDENT, who should be a Mechanical Engineer.**
> * **E** **METALLURGIST.**
> **F** **MECHANICAL ENGINEER.**
> **G** **MECHANICAL ENGINEER.**

III   The duties of the following relate almost entirely to the Cash and Stores and to the Book-keeping and Office Work generally, see Account Books Nos **1** to **9**

> **ACCOUNTANT AND CASHIER.**
> **WAGES CLERK.**
> **STORES CLERK OR STORE KEEPER.**

In drafting the list of officers as above, a perfectly full complement has been given , and in specifying the records required from each man in the different Forms **A** to **G**, it is assumed that there is a separate head for each department

If, however as already mentioned the work of two or more departments is managed by one officer for the sake of economy, as may be necessary in small Mines, the records of each department should nevertheless, be kept separate on the special forms provided in this book

Any changes the Manager may desire to make must be made in harmony with the above design   The system lends itself to local variation, and is sufficiently elastic to admit of changes, provided they are made advisedly

All such variations in the arrangements should be definitely advised to the Head Office, and, when approved, should be entered in this book with the date of approval

FOR GOLD MINING BUSINESS.

The following is a list of the staff, *arranged according to the special technical training of each Member, for the different departments of the work.* The juniors in each section are the natural successors to the seniors, on vacancies occurring, and if they are otherwise competent, should be promoted accordingly :—

MINING ENGINEERING STAFF.

GENERAL MANAGER.
MINE ENGINEER OR MINE SURVEYOR.
MINE FOREMAN OR CAPTAIN.

METALLURGICAL STAFF.

METALLURGIST.
ASSAYER.

MECHANICAL ENGINEERING STAFF.

MECHANICAL SUPERINTENDENT.
MILL SUPERINTENDENT.

BUSINESS STAFF.

COMMERCIAL SUPERINTENDENT OR MINE SECRETARY.
ACCOUNTANT AND CASHIER.
WAGES CLERK.
STORES CLERK OR STORE KEEPER.

The General Manager must report yearly to the Board on the efficiency of each member of the staff.

Specimens.—On pages 9 to 14 are given the usual Engagement Forms for :—
GENERAL MANAGER.
STAFF.
WORKMEN.

Notes.—The following notes may be found useful when entering into an engagement with employés :—

NOTE No. 1.—The General Manager usually requires to be provided with a Power of Attorney which should be drawn up by the Solicitor of the Company.

NOTE No. 2.—If the Company's name is inserted the Agreement must be sealed, and a 10/ stamp is required. If an official is made a party to the Agreement, and signs on behalf of the Company, only a 6d. stamp is required.

NOTE No. 3.—The rules should be annexed to the Agreement, and signed by the employé. If any degree of good organization is to be attained, general rules of some kind—for instance, the rules under the headings of the Departmental Reports in this book—may be used, or some modification or improvement thereof.

NOTE No. 4.—In cases where it is necessary for an Assistant to have charge of money, and to obtain a monetary guarantee for fidelity, suitable clauses should be added to the Agreement for these purposes, drawn up by a Solicitor.

NOTE No. 5.—If an official is made a party to the Agreement, this clause will run thus :—" As Witness the hands of the said Assistant and the said *official* on behalf of the Company."

NOTE No. 6.—Any variation from the printed form should be added at the end of the forms, or on margins, as the forms thus altered admit of the variations from the usual terms of engagement being more readily seen than when a completely new form is printed or written out.

Articles of Agreement made and entered into this *Second* day of *September* One thousand *nine* hundred and *three* between *A B Company Limited* whose Registered Office is at *Cannon Street, London, E C* (hereinafter called the Company), of the one part, and *John Smith* of *Newcastle, England,* (hereinafter called the General Manager), of the other part

The Company hereby agrees to engage the General Manager who hereby agrees to enter into and continue in the service of the Company as General Manager of the Company in for and during the term of *two years,* to commence from his arrival at the Company's mines, and thenceforward continuously until his engagement is terminated, as hereinafter provided on the conditions following —that is to say,

1 — The General Manager shall proceed to the Company's property at *in the district of* by *Steamer, leaving England not later than* , and immediately on his arrival there and while he shall continue in the service of the Company, shall faithfully and diligently serve the Company as General Manager, as aforesaid, to the best of his knowledge and ability, at such place or places in to which he may from time to time be directed to proceed by the Board of Directors of the Company

2 — He shall devote his whole time and attention, with zeal and energy, to the due and faithful performance of his duties under this Agreement, and shall use his utmost exertions to promote the business and interests of the Company during the continuance of this Agreement, and shall not at any time absent himself from the service of the Company, nor from the due and regular performance of his said duties, unless unavoidably prevented by illness or with the previous consent of the Board of Directors of the Company, and shall not at any time hereafter divulge or make known any of the trusts, secrets, processes dealings or accounts of or relating to the said business, or to the affairs of the Company, but shall keep the same undisclosed and inviolate

3 — He shall in all things be subservient to and obey the orders and directions of the Board of Directors of the Company in relation to the said business and shall not during the continuance of this Agreement, directly or indirectly, alone or in partnership, be connected with or concerned in any other business than that of the Company, or be engaged in any capacity whatsoever other than in the service of the Company and shall not engage in any speculation, business, mining, inspecting or prospecting for account of himself or others, without the previous consent and written authority of the Board of Directors   And in the event of any breach of this Agreement, he shall pay the Company the sum of £ as and for liquidated and ascertained damages for each such breach

4 — He shall attend to the rules for reporting all particulars necessary to shew the operations at the mines so far as he is capable of furnishing the same, as specified on the official forms laid down by the Company, and shall not make any alteration nor depart from the system and forms without the consent of the Board of Directors

5 — The Company shall during the continuance of this Agreement, and provided the General Manager shall duly observe and perform the agreements on his part, herein contained, pay to the General Manager the sum of per annum as salary, and so in proportion for any less period than a year, by equal monthly payments, on the usual pay day of each month to commence from the date of his arrival at the Company's property

6 — The Company shall provide the General Manager with a free passage *first* class to such place as he shall be required to proceed, and also house accommodation   But board and all other personal expenses are to be defrayed by the General Manager

7.——This Agreement shall continue in force after the expiry of the period herein named unless either party give notice to the other party of the intention to terminate this Agreement and the engagement hereby made, by giving or sending by post, in a registered letter to the other party hereto, *three* calendar months' notice in writing; such notice to be given or sent to the Company at their said Registered Office, or to the General Manager at his usual or last known place of abode; and at the expiration of such *three* calendar months from the giving or sending of such notice, the said engagement and this Agreement shall determine. Provided always that the Company may, in lieu of such notice, determine the said Agreement at any time on payment to the General Manager of *three* months' salary in advance.

8.——In the event of the General Manager leaving the Company's service after a period of *two years* from the time he enters upon his duties on the Company's property in   and duly observing the agreements herein contained, on his part, the Company, provided he returns to England forthwith, shall pay the expense of his return journey, which shall not exceed £

9.——If the General Manager shall at any time neglect or refuse, or become or be unable, whether on the ground of illness or otherwise, to perform or comply with all or any of the Articles of this Agreement, or any of the duties required of him, or all or any of the orders of the Board of Directors of the Company, or if he shall in any manner misconduct himself, or shall transact any business for his own account alone, or jointly with or for the account of any other person or persons, company or companies, or if he employ himself in any capacity whatsoever, other than in the sole employ of the Company, without the previous consent and written authority of the Board of Directors of the Company, it shall be lawful for the Board of Directors of the Company to terminate the engagement of the General Manager forthwith without giving any such notice or payment in advance as aforesaid; and immediately thereupon the salary and every other payment which the General Manager may then or might thereafter be entitled to receive, and all benefit and advantage whatsoever to be derived by him under or by virtue of this Agreement, shall cease. Provided always that if the health of the General Manager should break down through no fault of his own, and a medical certificate be given by the Board's Doctor to that effect, the Company shall pay the cost of his return journey to England.

It is hereby, lastly, agreed between the parties hereto, that this Agreement shall, in all respects, be construed and carried into effect according to the law of England, so far as may be and the circumstances will permit.

In Witness whereof the Company has caused its Common Seal to be hereunto affixed, and   *John Smith*   has hereunto set his hand and seal the day and year first above written.

} *Directors.*

Secretary.

Seal of Company.

Witness to the signature of the
said *John Smith,*

James Black, *Witness.* }

John Smith.

𝕬𝖗𝖙𝖎𝖈𝖑𝖊𝖘 𝖔𝖋 𝕬𝖌𝖗𝖊𝖊𝖒𝖊𝖓𝖙 made and entered into this *second* day of *September*, One thousand *nine* hundred and *three* between *James White* on behalf of *A B Company Limited* whose Registered Office is at *Cannon Street, London, & C* (hereinafter called the Company), of the one part, and *John Clark* of (hereinafter called the Assistant) of the other part

The Company hereby agrees to engage the Assistant, who hereby agrees to enter into and continue in the service of the Company in as *Clerk and Storekeeper* for and during the term of *two years* to commence from his arrival at the Company's property, and thenceforward continuously until his engagement is terminated as hereinafter provided, on the conditions following —that is to say,

1 The Assistant shall proceed to the Company's property at *in the district of* by *Steamer leaving England not later than* , and while he shall continue in the service of the Company, shall faithfully and diligently serve the Company as aforesaid, or in any other suitable capacity in which he may be required by the General Manager or other duly authorized officer of the Company (hereinafter called the Company's Officer) to make his services available in the transaction of the business of the Company, to the best of his knowledge and ability at such place or places in to which he may from time to time be directed to proceed by the Company's Officer

2 —He shall devote his whole time and attention, with zeal and energy, to the due and faithful performance of his duties under this Agreement, and shall use his utmost exertions to promote the business and interests of the Company during the continuance of this Agreement, and shall not at any time absent himself from the service of the Company, nor from the due and regular performance of his said duties, unless unavoidably prevented by illness, or with the previous consent of the Company's Officer, and shall not at any time hereafter divulge or make known any of the trusts, secrets, processes, dealings, or accounts of or relating to the said business, or to the affairs of the Company, but shall keep the same undisclosed and inviolate

3 —He shall in all things be subservient to and obey the orders and directions of the Company's Officer in relation to the said business, and shall not, during the continuance of this Agreement, directly or indirectly, alone or in partnership, be connected with or concerned in any other business than that of the Company, or be engaged in any capacity whatsoever other than in the service of the Company, and shall not engage in any speculation, business, mining, inspecting or prospecting for account of himself or others, without the previous consent and written authority of the Board of Directors And in the event of any breach of this Agreement, he shall pay the Company the sum of Fifty Pounds as and for liquidated and ascertained damages for each such breach

4 —He shall attend to the rules for reporting all particulars necessary to shew the operations of the department in which he is engaged so far as he is capable of furnishing the same, as specified on the official forms laid down by the Company for such department, and shall not make any alteration nor depart from the system and forms without the consent of the Board of Directors

5 —The Company shall, during the continuance of this Agreement, and provided the Assistant shall duly observe and perform the agreements on his part, herein contained, pay to the Assistant the sum of per annum as salary, and so in proportion for any less period than a year, by equal monthly payments on the usual pay day of each month to commence from the date of his arrival at the Company's property

6 - The Company shall provide the Assistant with a free passage *second* class,

to such place as he shall be required by the Company's Officer to proceed. Staff Quarters will be provided, but board and all other personal expenses are to be defrayed by the Assistant.

7.—This agreement shall continue in force after the expiry of the period herein named unless either party give notice to the other party of the intention to terminate this Agreement and the engagement hereby made, by giving or sending by post, in a registered letter to the other party hereto, *three* calendar months' notice in writing; such notice to be given or sent to the Company at their said Registered Office, or to the Assistant at his usual or last known place of abode; and at the expiration of such *three* calendar months from the giving or sending of such notice, the said engagement and this Agreement shall determine. Provided always that the Company may, in lieu of such notice, determine the said Agreement at any time on payment to the Assistant of *three* months' salary in advance.

8.—In the event of the Assistant leaving the Company's service after a period of *two years* from the time he enters upon his duties on the Company's property in and duly observing the agreements herein contained, on his part, the Company, provided he returns to England forthwith, shall pay the expense of his return journey, which shall not exceed £.

9.—If the Assistant shall at any time neglect or refuse, or become or be unable, whether on the ground of illness or otherwise, to perform or comply with all or any of the Articles of this Agreement, or any of the duties required of him, or all or any of the orders of the Company's Officer, or if he shall in any manner misconduct himself, or shall transact any business for his own account alone, or jointly with or for the account of any other person or persons, company or companies, or if he employ himself in any capacity whatsoever, other than in the sole employ of the Company, without the previous consent and written authority of the Board of Directors of the Company, it shall be lawful for the Board of Directors of the Company or for the Company's Officer to terminate the engagement of the Assistant forthwith without giving any such notice or payment in advance as aforesaid; and immediately thereupon the salary and every other payment which the Assistant may then or might thereafter be entitled to receive, and all benefit and advantage whatsoever to be derived by him under or by virtue of this Agreement shall cease. Provided always that if the health of the Assistant should break down through no fault of his own, and a medical certificate be given by the Board's Doctor to that effect, the Company shall pay the expense of his return journey to England.

It is hereby, lastly, agreed between the parties hereto, that this Agreement shall, in all respects, be construed and carried into effect according to the law of England, so far as may be and the circumstances will permit.

As Witness the hands of the Company's Officer and of the said Assistant, the day and year first above written.

Signed by the said
in the presence of

6d. Stamp.

Articles of Agreement

made and entered into this *second* day of *September,* One thousand *nine* hundred and *three* between *James White* on behalf of *A B Company Limited,* whose Registered Office is at *Cannon Street, London, E C* (hereinafter called the Company), of the one part, and *Peter Reid* of (hereinafter called the Workman), of the other part

The Company hereby agrees to engage the Workman, who hereby agrees to enter into and continue in the service of the Company in as *Miner* for and during the term of *two years* to commence from his arrival at the Company's property, and thenceforward continuously until his engagement is terminated, as hereinafter provided on the conditions following —that is to say,

1 —The Workman shall proceed to the Company's property at *in the district of* , by *Steamer leaving England not later than* and while he shall continue in the service of the Company, shall faithfully and diligently serve the Company as aforesaid, or in any other suitable capacity in which he may be required by the General Manager or other duly authorized officer of the Company (hereinafter called the Company's Officer), to make his services available in the transaction of the business of the Company to the best of his knowledge and ability, at such place or places in to which he may from time to time be directed to proceed by the Company's Officer

2 —He shall devote his whole time and attention, with zeal and energy, to the due and faithful performance of his duties under this Agreement, and shall use his utmost exertions to promote the business and interests of the Company during the continuance of this Agreement, and shall not at any time absent himself from the service of the Company, nor from the due and regular performance of his said duties unless unavoidably prevented by illness, or with the previous consent of the Company's Officer and shall not at any time hereafter divulge or make known any of the trusts, secrets, processes dealings or accounts of or relating to the said business, or to the affairs of the Company, but shall keep the same undisclosed and inviolate

3 —He shall in all things be subservient to and obey the orders and directions of the Company's Officer in relation to the said business, and shall not, during the continuance of this Agreement, directly or indirectly, alone or in partnership be connected with or concerned in any other business than that of the Company or be engaged in any capacity whatsoever other than in the service of the Company, and shall not engage in any speculation, business, mining, inspecting or prospecting for account of himself or others, without the previous consent and written authority of the Board of Directors And in the event of any breach of this Agreement he shall pay the Company the sum of Twenty-five Pounds as and for liquidated and ascertained damages for each such breach

4 —The Company shall, during the continuance of this Agreement, and provided the Workman shall duly observe and perform the agreements, on his part, herein contained, pay to him the sum of per annum as wages, and so in proportion for any less period than a year, by equal monthly payments, on the usual pay day of each month, to commence from the date of his arrival at the Company's property

5 —The Company shall provide the Workman with a free passage, third class to such place as he shall be required by the Company's Officer to proceed Workmen's Quarters will be provided but board and all other personal expenses are to be defrayed by the Workman

6 —This Agreement shall continue in force after the expiry of the period herein named unless either party give notice to the other party of the intention to terminate this Agreement and the engagement hereby made, by giving or sending by post, in a registered letter to the other party hereto, *three* calendar months' notice in writing, such notice to be given or sent to the Company at their said Registered Office, or to the

Workman at his usual or last known place of abode ; and at the expiration of such *three* calendar months from the giving or sending of such notice, the said engagement and this Agreement shall determine. Provided always that the Company may, in lieu of such notice, determine the said Agreement at any time on payment to the Workman of *three* months' wages in advance.

7.——In the event of the Workman leaving the Company's service after a period of *two years* from the time he enters upon his duties on the Company's property in and duly observing the agreements herein contained, on his part, the Company, provided he returns to England forthwith, shall pay the expense of his return journey, which shall not exceed pounds.

8.——If the Workman shall at any time neglect or refuse, or become or be unable, whether on the ground of illness or otherwise, to perform or comply with all or any of the Articles of this Agreement, or any of the duties required of him, or all or any of the orders of the Company's Officer, or if he shall in any manner misconduct himself, or shall transact any business for his own account alone, or jointly with or for the account of any other person or persons, company or companies, or if he employ himself in any capacity whatsoever, other than in the sole employ of the Company, without the previous consent and written authority of the Board of Directors of the Company, it shall be lawful for the Board of Directors of the Company or for the Company's Officer to terminate the engagement of the Workman forthwith without giving any such notice or payment in advance as aforesaid ; and immediately thereupon the salary and every other payme..t which he may then or might thereafter be entitled to receive, and all benefit and advantage whatsoever to be derived by him under or by virtue of this Agreement, shall cease. Provided always that if the health of the Workman should break down through no fault of his own, and a medical certificate be given by the Board's Doctor to that effect, the Company shall pay the expense of his return journey to England.

It is hereby, lastly, agreed between the parties hereto, that this Agreement shall, in all respects, be construed and carried into effect according to the law of England, so far as may be and the circumstances will permit.

As Witness the hands of the Company's Officer and of the said Workman the day and year first above written.

Signed by the said
   in the presence of

6d. Stamp.

FOREMEN.

In addition to the staff already mentioned, there are also the Foremen of the various sub-departments, whose duties are to superintend and keep the time of the men employed in the works.

The following is a specimen of the Wages Time Book:—

𝔚𝔞𝔤𝔢𝔰 𝔗𝔦𝔪𝔢 𝔅𝔬𝔬𝔨 (*kept by Foremen*).

Month of .... *19* .... *Department.*

Name.	Rate.													

The Foremen should be carefully instructed as to the departmental headings required in the Wages Sheet (see page 145).

It will usually happen that each department has a Foreman, so that the whole of that Foreman's gang will be debited to that department, unless in cases where men have been transferred to another department for a short time; in which cases care must be taken to see that the men are not twice paid.

When employing Natives the Time Ticket is usually adopted. The Native keeps the Ticket, and his time is marked upon it as worked.

The following is a specimen of the Ticket:—

NATIVE TIME CARD.

No. ....

Name, ...   *Date,* *19*

M.	Tu.	W.	Th.	F.	S.	Days.	Where and How Employed.

Rate, ...   *Amount,* ....

The Foremen also write the orders for goods which may be required from the Store. The following is a specimen :—

ORDER BOOK (*used by Foremen*).	
No.	....................................*19* No. ....
.... *19*	.... *Works.*
.... *Dept.*	*To the* **STORES CLERK.**
....	*Please deliver to* ....*Department*
....	....
....	....
....	....
.... *Foreman.*	.... *Foreman.*

Full instructions regarding Foremen should be specially written out by the Manager, or by the Superintendent of the department, for the approval of the General Manager.

The Foremen should also be provided with Note Books, into which should be entered all memoranda which it is necessary for them to keep.

REQUISITIONS FOR CASH TO BE SUPPLIED BY THE HEAD OFFICE.

Estimate

An estimate to be made of the total amount required for each month, and regularly transmitted to the Head Office in ample time to make provision for the amount required

The efficient control of expenditure will be much aided by a systematic allocation of funds to different departments before they are spent   A forecast or " Budget " should be required from the responsible officers, so that as far as possible expenditure may be approved before, and not after, it is incurred and that funds may be provided in due time   Neglect of this precaution has often landed Companies in financial difficulties which might have been avoided

Authority

To be signed by the General Manager and/or the Commercial Superintendent, as may be specially arranged by the Board

To be copied in Letter Book, titled REQUISITIONS TO HEAD OFFICE

Letter Book copies of these requisitions should be kept in preference to counterfoils

REQUISITIONS FOR STORES TO BE SUPPLIED BY THE HEAD OFFICE.

Estimate.

As in the case of Cash, an estimate List of Stores required, which are to be supplied from the Head Office, should be made up regularly, and a requisition sent to the Head Office in ample time for them to be forwarded.

In order to keep the General Manager apprised of what Stores are required when stocks run low, a list should be regularly supplied by the Stores Clerk to the Manager, so that he can order what is necessary.

Specimen.

The following is a usual specimen for such a Form:

(NAME OF THE COMPANY.)

Requisition for Stores, No.

....*190*

Please supply the following:—

No.	DESCRIPTION.

Authority.

The General Manager and/or the Commercial Superintendent, as may be specially arranged by the Board, should sign each requisition.

To be Copied in Letter Book, titled REQUISITIONS TO HEAD OFFICE.

Letter Book copies of these requisitions should be kept in preference to counterfoils.

ORDERS FOR STORES TO LOCAL MERCHANTS.

All Stores which it may be found can be advantageously obtained locally, are to be so ordered.

Specimen.

The following is a usual specimen of an Order Form :—

(NAME OF THE COMPANY.)

Order No.

.... *190*

Please supply the following :—

No.	DESCRIPTION.				

Authority.

All orders are to be signed by the General Manager and/or the Commercial Superintendent, as specially arranged by the Board.

To be Copied in Letter Book, titled "ORDERS TO LOCAL MERCHANTS."

Correspondence.

After each order is signed all subsequent correspondence as to forwarding, delivery, &c., should be carried out and signed by the Commercial Superintendent.

Invoices.

These should be duly compared, as to quantity and price, with the order as given in this book. See reference to this on page 95.

Current Prices of Stores.

A book with this information should be kept for reference.

Cheques.

The General Manager, in conjunction with the Commercial Superintendent, signs the cheques for payment of the goods.

Copies for the Head Office.

A press copy of each contract or order, say over £100 in amount, to be sent to the Office.

FOR GOLD MINING BUSINESS.

SPACE RESERVED FOR MS. NOTES.

CORRESPONDENCE.

Head Office Letters.

A letter should be sent to the Head Office by the General Manager every week respecting the technical and working affairs of the Company, and a letter should also be sent by the Commercial Superintendent every week giving reports on matters under his supervision

Legal Correspondence.

The Commercial Superintendent should bring before the General Manager all legal business and the Manager should arrange with the Commercial Superintendent the course to be adopted   Letters on such business should always be signed by the Manager

Authority

When it is necessary for the General Manager to be absent he should leave specific instructions for the Commercial Superintendent to sign any letters and orders in his absence, such letters to be signed under the phrase "For the General Manager"   On his return he should read such letters over, and initial them in Copy Letter Book   Except in special cases, when letters are marked Private, all other correspondence either outgoing or incoming, is open to both General Manager and the Commercial Superintendent

The Letter Books

The Books already referred to on previous pages, and those required for the above correspondence, are as follows —

A   Requisitions to Head Office for Cash and Stores

B   Orders to Local Merchants

C   London or Head Office Letters

D   Letters to Local Merchants and Forwarding Agents

E   General and Legal Letters

REGISTER OF LETTERS RECEIVED.

It is of much importance in a business of this kind to have a Register of Letters Received kept in a systematic manner, so that there may be no evasion of facts or suppression of information, all of which is the property of the Company.

Specimen.

The following is the usual form of such a book :—

Register of Letters Received,					
Date Received.	Date of Letter.	Consecutive Number.	From	Subject.	Answered.

Responsible Officer.—The Commercial Superintendent.

REGISTER OF PLANS.

As in the case of Letters, a Register of Plans Received should be kept in a systematic manner, so that there may be no evasion of facts or suppression of information; all of which is the property of the Company.

Specimen.

In large concerns it may be found to be of advantage to have a book for entries made in chronological order as received, of which the following is a specimen :—

Register of Plans,

Date Received or Completed.	No. as Received.	No. of Letter of Advice.	DESCRIPTION.	From Whom Received.	No. as Arranged in Head Office	REMARKS.

Another book should be provided for indexing in detail under the following heads :—

TOPOGRAPHICAL PLANS.
GEOLOGICAL PLANS.
MINING PLANS.
PROGRESS PLANS.
MECHANICAL PLANS.

These headings are all self-explanatory.

The Machinery Templates, and Gauges are also to be registered in this book as a separate part.

Specimen.

The following is a usual specimen of such book :—

Index of Plans,

Date Received or Completed.	No. as Received.	Consecutive Arranged Number.	No. of Letter of Advice.	DESCRIPTION.	DRAWN BY	REMARKS.

Responsible Officers.

The Manager should arrange, in some convenient way, that plans from all departments should be registered in this book.

This book is kept in sections by the officials as may be arranged by the Manager.

All Plans sent to Head Office should always be numbered consecutively.

Directions for Plans.

On pages 25 and 26 will be found suitable rules for obtaining uniformity in Plans.

DIRECTIONS FOR PLANS.

System of Reference by Squares

All drawings are, as a rule, to be made upon paper of double elephant size It will be convenient, in the case of survey plans, plans of mine workings &c, to adopt a systematic method of reference to such plans so that, for instance small tracings sent home to illustrate any particular point, and progress tracings, can be readily and accurately fitted on to the duplicate plans maintained in the London Office

To do this, the sheet should be divided into squares of exactly 6 inches in the side by fine horizontal and vertical lines The sheet being 42 inches long, there will be seven columns of squares in the length numbered from left to right 1 to 7 The width is 27 inches, which gives four horizontal rows of squares, to be lettered from top to bottom, **A, B, C, D**, and there will be 3 inches over, which can be left as a margin of 1½ inches top and bottom, thus—

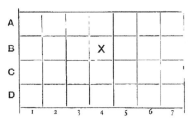

Now, if it be required to send home a tracing of some portion of the plan included within the square marked ⟦x⟧, it will only be necessary to shew on the tracing the index lines enclosing that square and to state that it is square No 4 **B** on such and such a drawing The tracing can then be placed in its exact position on the London plan, and the new work fitted on to the old with accuracy

Surveys.

It will greatly facilitate the extension of surveys in the future, and the fitting together of new with old work if, in the first place an accurate skeleton survey be made of the whole ground over which any detail plans are likely to be required afterwards, the skeleton survey being made merely to fix permanently the position of a few points and lines, which can afterwards be used as bases on which to tie the interior detail surveys In short, the surveys should be elaborated from the outside inwards, not from the inside outwards For a skeleton a trigonometrical survey from a carefully-measured base line is best, but very fair accuracy can be obtained by enclosing the ground within a polygon, surveyed with a good compass and chain, if the errors be distributed over the circuit by working out the latitudes and departures on the traverse system, and apportioning the errors among the sides of the polygon

Sections.

In cases where deep workings are in use, and sectional plans are required to elucidate progress, an application of the index system used for survey plans will be advantageous

Section paper, containing 6 squares to the inch, can be obtained in con tinuous rolls 54 inches wide, besides the margin This can therefore be cut in lengths of 74 inches, which will be the standard double elephant size

-35-

Each of these may be divided by lines into 28 squares of 6 inches square, numbered and lettered as in the case of survey plans. On a scale of 40 feet to 1 inch, each of the small divisions of this paper ($\frac{1}{8}$ inch) represents 5 feet, and will therefore shew levels, cross-cuts, &c., distinctly. As 1 foot on this scale represents 480 feet, and the paper shrinks a little, the scale is sufficiently near $\frac{1}{500}$ natural to compare fairly well with a surface plan on that scale; but the horizontal plan of underground workings should be shewn on the section paper above or below the sectional plan; the width of the paper gives plenty of room for this on the 40' scale.

For details requiring a larger scale, the same section paper can be used for a scale of 16 feet to the inch, which is very near $\frac{1}{200}$ natural.

Scales.

In all cases it is desirable to adopt natural scales— $\frac{1}{50}$, $\frac{1}{500}$, $\frac{1}{5000}$, or as the case may be—because dimensions can be read off such drawings in any desired system of measurement—English, French, Dutch, &c. In addition to the scale usually shewn upon plans, the scale used should be described in words.

Datum.

A permanent datum should be established from the first, to which all levels should be referred. When levels have been brought up from the sea level, the datum should be a fixed number of feet above sea level. If this is not available, some permanent, indestructible, and easily identified bench mark should be established, and all levels connected with it.

For mining sections it is more convenient to reckon reduced levels downwards from a datum line in the air, than from one below upwards, as in railway or hydraulic surveys.

The reduced levels will then read the same way as the depths of shafts, &c. This, of course, does not prevent the datum line being assumed at a fixed number of feet above sea level; but the reduced levels will be x feet (or metres) below datum instead of above it.

North Point.

Every plan should have the true north or meridian shewn upon it if possible; but if the variation is not known, and only the magnetic meridian can be given, it should be so described on the plan.

Natural Scales.

As there is sometimes a difficulty in obtaining natural scales suitably arranged for plotting from measurements taken in feet, it may be well to mention that a set of such scales specially designed for surface and underground work by the writer of these notes, can be obtained from Mr. W. F. Stanley, Railway Approach, London Bridge, London, S.E. They may be ordered as "Elwes' Natural Scales, Nos. 1 to 4."

REGISTER OF SAMPLES RECEIVED TO BE ASSAYED.

Samples of all kinds of ore and tailings should be taken according to arrangements made by the General Manager, such as are specially adapted to the circumstances of each case. In making his arrangements he will be guided to some extent by the specimens given on the following pages.

All manual labour required in connection with sampling will be specially arranged by the Manager.

In the discretion of the Manager, the sampling is to be done either by the Assayer or some one else appointed by the Manager. All samples to be registered in a book kept for the purpose.

Specimen.

The following is a usual copy for such a book :—

Register of Samples Received for Assay.

Number.	Date Received.	DESCRIPTION.	From Whom Received.	Determination to be made.	Date When Finished.

After a sample has been once drawn, representing any particular quantity of ore—say 100 tons—the assay should be made on this sample. It is irregular to mix samples, say of two lots of 100 tons each, and make one assay for the 200 tons, as it has been found in practice that such a method does not give exact results. If it is considered that 200 ton lot samples are sufficient, then the samples must be drawn as representing the 200 tons ; or they may be made upon larger lots, as may be considered desirable.

Entries for this Book.

The samples received are to be carefully labelled, numbered, and registered in this book.

Responsible Officer.—The Assayer.

Directions for Sampling.

On the following pages, 29 to 35, are specimens of Sampling Methods under the following heads :—

Samples taken of Surface Exposures.
Samples of Ore taken in various kinds of Ore Bodies.
Samples of Ore taken from the Mine and passed into Process.
Samples taken during stages of Process.
Samples taken of Bullion Produced.

These are the classes of samples which fall to be registered.

If any samples are taken to be assayed for a neighbouring Company, they must be specially marked ; and any assays so done must be charged for.

Employés are not allowed to assay any samples for their own account.

FOR GOLD MINING BUSINESS.

SPACE RESERVED FOR MS. NOTES.

SAMPLING.*

HOW SAMPLES SHOULD BE TAKEN OF SURFACE EXPOSURES OF GOLD-BEARING ROCKS, SURFACE FLOAT, AND IN PROSPECTING WORK GENERALLY.

The primary form of all prospecting in a suspected gold-bearing belt of country is, necessarily, to pan the alluvial wash found in its valleys, creeks, or river beds.

A series of pannings along the alluvial patches, formed from the disintegration and denudation of the adjacent hills and uplands, will reveal the existence of Gold if it has formed up in the rocks within the drainage area of the district.

If Gold is found to exist, search may be instituted for the containing reefs; and the value of the various outcrops, float, and exposures, which may be ultimately found along the line of the reef, must be determined as a guide to more extended search and exploratory work in depth.

In the absence of solid outcrops of reef, from which to determine the line of reef in direction, attention should be directed to any patches of quartz float to be seen. If a series of these patches of quartz float is discovered, it will be more conducive to orderly working to connect them on a rough map, from a preliminary survey. Once in position on the map, an intelligent observer will be able to decide if they form along the line of one main reef, or form separate and independent bodies.

Let it be assumed, first, that they form the surface indications of one main reef. The point to be determined, in the first place, is the value of each patch, treated separately.

The sampling will be conducted at right angles to the axis of the float patch, or, in any case, at right angles to the supposed line of reef underlying or adjacent to it. The various samples, taken in this way along the axis of the patch, should be equi-distant from each other. The actual distance, in feet, between them must be determined by the length of the patch—for a small patch, say every 20 feet; and for a larger patch, 50 feet may be found suitable.

In the taking of the sample as little as possible should be left to the judgment of the sampler, in taking one piece of float quartz or in rejecting another. To provide against this difficulty the following plan is suggested:—Four thin cotton or hemp lines, parallel to and equi-distant from each other 12 inches, should be stretched across the part of the float patch to be sampled, and at right angles to its axis, and made tight with pegs on either side. On each of these lines let there be a red cotton tag every 9 inches or thereby. The disposition of the strings and red markers are as shewn on the diagram:—

QUARTZ FLOAT.

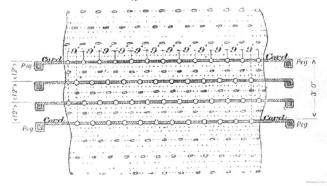

* The ... Mr. ... Ferguson for the Specimens of Ru... for Sampling and the ... sketches up to page 33.

It will be seen that the red markers on one line are not directly opposite those of the adjacent, but of the alternate line. The sampler begins on the first line, and picks up a small piece of quartz float at each of the red tags, and repeats the same thing at the red marks of the other three lines. The float from all the lines are now put together and ground up in the usual way, and afterwards rolled on a glazed cotton cloth, cut and quartered until the sample is down to the required quantity. It is then put into a canvas bag, the number of which is registered in the Sample Book, for reference at any time if successive assays of the sample should be required.

A series of assays, made from samples taken in the manner described above, at regular intervals along the quartz float patch, will give the value of the patch as a whole, and the individual assays will shew the good and the poor places in it.

In the same way, the mean of all the assays made from samples of the different patches will give the surface assay value of the reef, and the average assay value of each patch independently will shew where the reef is highest in value.

From the accumulated information thus obtained, the position, extent, and character of the exploratory work to prove the reef in depth and in value can be determined with considerable accuracy. In the absence of such bold and infallible indications as gold-bearing reef outcrops or ancient works, the prospector must fall back on surface indications, such as quartz float, and make his judgments rest on the evidence carefully obtained from them.

Sampling reef outcrops should just be done every way the same as that described for reef sampling in depth on the following page, so that the rules laid down for the one will apply equally to the other.

The more assays made from correctly-made samples, over a reef exposure, outcrop, or reserve, in regular sequence, the more likely is the mean of the total number to approximate to the actual assay value of the whole ore body.

SAMPLING—continued

HOW SAMPLES SHOULD BE TAKEN OF ORE FOR AVERAGE ASSAY VALUES OF THE ORE IN RESERVES, IN STOPES AND GALLERIES OF THE MINE

The sample should invariably represent, as accurately as possible, the average value of the ore at the point sampled, and the system of sampling which will give this result, with the least handling or selection of the sampler, is the most reliable

As far as possible the hand of the sampler ought not to touch any individual part of the ore forming the sample, as, in doing so, a piece of ore may either be added to or rejected from the sample, which materially alters its value and renders the average assay value obtained from it unreliable and incorrect

The sampler should work with tools only in taking his samples, and these are few and simple A pick, a gad and a hammer, with a piece of cotton preferably glazed black on one side for catching the ore as it falls from the stroke of the tools, are his full requirements By careful cutting on the part of the sampler any ore, lumps, incrustations, or powdered ore falling into the cotton sheet held under his tools, will represent the average of the ore body at the point operated on Whatever falls into the cotton sheet should be ground up fine before any part of it is taken for assay by cutting and quartering

Samples should be taken along a line at right angles to the dip of the ore body, or, what is the same thing, at right angles to its hanging and foot walls They should also be taken from the roof or sides of the galleries and stopes, in preference to the floor on account of the facility of catching in the cotton sheet all the ore that falls away from the tools of the sampler

Where the ore is very uniform in composition one line of sampling, cut across the ore body at right angles to its dip, may represent a correct average of the value of the ore at that part of the gallery or stope Much more frequently however it will be found that it does not and to guard against such possibilities the sampler should have every such sample composed of the cuttings from three lines, running at right angles to the walls of the ore body These three lines should be equi-distant from each other, and, if possible, not less than 1½ foot to 2 feet apart

SAMPLES TAKEN FROM THE ROOF —This is the place to be taken where possible then the three lines will represent a reliable average of 4½ feet to 6 feet of the ore body along its strike, and its thickness so far as exposed

SAMPLES TAKEN FROM THE FACE OF A LEVEL —Then the three lines will represent a reliable average of 4½ to 6 feet along the dip of the ore body, and its thickness so far as exposed

SAMPLES TAKEN FROM THE SIDE OF A CROSS-CUT —The three lines will represent a reliable average of 4½ to 6 feet along the dip of the ore body, and its thickness, so far as exposed and if the sides of two adjacent cross-cuts are sampled in this way, the mean of the two will represent a fair average of 4½ to 6 feet high by the thickness of the ore body between its containing walls, or so far as exposed, and by the length between the cross-cuts

In this way it will be observed that a sample from one line, across the ore body, represents an assay value in position only A sample from the roof or face of a level in three lines, represents a value in area, while a sample, the mean of two sides, and three lines in each, across a cross cut, represents the value in volume or cubical contents

Preferably, however, samples taken in three or more lines equi-distant from each other and parallel and at right angles to the walls of the ore body in the roof of the gallery or stope should be obtained By repeating the samplings in this way, at as uniform distances along the levels, winzes, rises and stopes in the ore body as possible, the mean of the collected assay results should give a fair average of the value of the ore body in reserve

The diagrams on this and on the next page will explain the conditions of ore distribution in the ore carrier, ore matrix or reef body, under which the various methods of sampling will operate to advantage.

ORE BODY OF UNIFORM COMPOSITION.

The diagram shews where, in an ore body, as described above, a single line cut across the ore body at right angles to its walls would give a fair average value of it. The assay from a sample obtained in this way would give a value in position only.

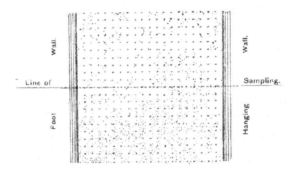

ORE BODY OF IRREGULAR COMPOSITION.

The diagram shews an ore body, as described above, where a single line sample would be likely to give an incorrect value, and where three or more lines of sampling at right angles to the walls of the ore body would approximate much more closely to the true value of the body, and would represent a value in area.

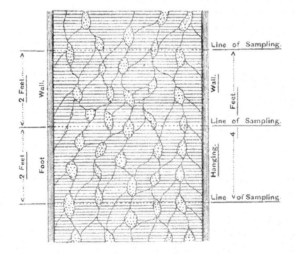

SAMPLING — continued.

ORE BODY OF IRREGULAR COMPOSITION, AND AT THE SAME TIME WITH THE ORE LYING AGAINST THE WALLS, WITH BARREN ROCK IN THE MIDDLE.

The diagram shews an ore body as described above. In such a case each side of the ore body might be sampled separately and treated as an independent body, but with the three or more lines across the short width selected for assay.

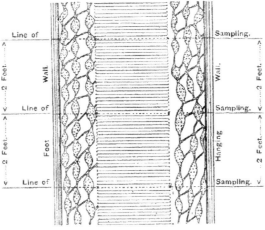

Ore Body.   Barren Reef.   Ore Body.

Supposing the sample is bulkier than desirable, it will still be the lesser evil to spend more time and work in grinding it up than attempting to reject any part of it previously.

Once ground up, the sample should be rolled along a black glazed cotton sheet, laid upon a flat table or floor. The rolling of the powdered ore, as distinguished from dragging it, should be alternately from right to left, and at right angles to it, to and from the operator.

In this way, by repeating the movements sufficiently, it will be found that the various streaks of colour running through the powdered ore at the beginning disappear, and one homogeneous shade pervades it. The ore may then be rolled into a round heap, approximating to a truncated cone, and cut into four divisions with a vertically held plate of ordinary window glass or thin sheet metal, squared at the edges, making two cuts at right angles to each other. This is called "Quartering."

QUARTERING.   QUARTERING AFTER SEPARATION.

This diagram shews how the quartering is done.

This diagram shews the quarters after being separated from each other.

Either the two corners hatched, diagonally opposite each other, or the other two corners should be taken, and again mixed and rolled together on the glazed cotton sheet, afterwards cut and quartered again, and the process repeated until the sample has reached the size required.

At this stage the sample should be placed in a bag with a number which is registered in the Sample Book at the Mine, and can be referred to when necessary.

SAMPLING—continued.

SAMPLING ARRANGEMENTS FOR ORE MINED AND PASSED INTO PROCESS.

WHERE THE SAMPLE IS TO BE TAKEN.

All ore going into or coming out of the stonebreaker must be carefully sampled.

QUANTITY OF ORE TO BE TAKEN AS THE SAMPLE.

From one in every twenty waggons, a shovelful, or other fixed quantity, to be set aside, in cases where the Gold is well distributed through the ore.

In cases where the Gold is unequally distributed, it is advisable to take from one waggon in every ten.

REDUCTION OF BULK OF THE SAMPLE.

The large sample having been thus selected and mixed, it should be reduced by dividing the heap into four, and proceeding as already described on page 33. It should finally be divided into two or three parts and put up in parcels, numbered (and sealed when necessary). One part is given to the Chemist to be assayed, and the others retained for reference.

BOTTLING AND SEALING THE SAMPLE.

Samples for transmission are to be put into bottles and sealed.

The foregoing rules also apply to sampling the ore as it passes through the various processes. This must be regularly and carefully done.

SAMPLING—continued.

SAMPLING ARRANGEMENTS FOR TAILINGS

TAILINGS FROM THE MILL

In sampling tailings from the Mill, the man on shift takes a dishful from each discharge launder every hour care being taken that there is no concentration of sands from slimes. All these samples are put into one bucket. At the end of twenty-four hours, a little alum or lime may be added and stirred up, and the whole then allowed to settle for a couple of hours.

When the sand or slime has settled the greater part of the water is poured off, and the remainder is passed through a filter of calico. The contents of the calico are then scraped on to a prospecting pan dried, and well mixed and sampled in the usual way by quartering.

TAILINGS CHARGED INTO VATS

In sampling tailings as they are being charged into the vats for cyanide treatment, every truck, as it enters the Cyanide Works, is sampled with an iron sampling-rod—a hollow rod, which brings away a core of sand after being pushed down into the centre of the truck. These samples so taken are shaken into a box placed beside each vat, and when the vat is full the contents of its sample box are thoroughly mixed up and quartered down by successive operations till the sample is reduced to about 2 lbs weight.

SPENT TAILINGS

Spent tailings or residues are dealt with exactly in the same way, the trucks as they leave the Works for the residue dump, being sampled with the rod.

OLD TAILINGS HEAPS

Old tailings heaps may be sampled either by the use of a sampling-rod, at points marked by the intersections of equi-distant lines drawn longitudinally and transversely across the surface of the heap, or by digging trenches across the heap, and taking every tenth or twentieth shovelful.

SAMPLING AND ASSAYING OF BULLION

See page 178

FOR GOLD MINING BUSINESS.

SPACE RESERVED FOR MS. NOTES.

REGISTER OF ASSAY RESULTS.

No samples are to be assayed except those specified in the Rules in the "Register of Samples" (see page 27).

Specimen.

The following is a usual specimen of such a book :—

Register of Assay Results.

Date when Finished.	Sample Number.	RESULTS OBTAINED.					REMARKS.
		Gold.	Silver.	Copper.	Bismuth.		

It is from this book that a Certificate of Assay can be given for the monthly results.

This Certificate should contain, in a condensed form, the information given in the "Register of Assay Results," and from this the assays in the Gold Account are obtained.

Specimen.

The following is the usual pattern, and a copy of which is to be sent to the Head Office :—

Assay Certificate *for Month of* ....

DATE.	No. of Sample.	Mark of Sample.	SOURCE OF SAMPLE.	GOLD per Ton of 2000 Lbs.			SILVER per Ton of 2000 Lbs.			DESCRIPTION & REMARKS.
				Ozs.	Dwts.	Grs.	Ozs.	Dwts.	Grs.	
			NOTE.—*In case of Bullion the weight of it must be given.*							

Responsible Officer.—The Assayer.

Entries for this Book.

Entries are only to be made of assays of the samples previously entered in the Register of Samples Received for Assay.

ORE IN SIGHT.

The methods of calculating "Ore in Sight" have hitherto lacked uniformity, and consequently the conclusions arrived at by different experts have varied widely when reporting on the same mine. The proposals of the INSTITUTION OF MINING AND METAL-LURGY that the data on which the calculations are made should be plainly stated, will do much to clear away such discrepancies. The following is a copy of their suggestions.

The Council of the INSTITUTION OF MINING AND METALLURGY recognizing the great importance, to the Mining Industry and to the public generally, of the subject dealt with in the *Paper* on "Ore in Sight," by Mr. J. D. KENDALL (*Transactions*, Volume X), appointed a Committee to consider what steps the Institution might usefully take in defining the term "Ore in Sight."

The views expressed by leading Members of the Profession shewed a great divergence of opinion as to the definition of the term.

After due consideration and discussion the Council came to the following decision :—

1. That Members of the Institution should not make use of the term "**Ore in Sight**," in their Reports, without indicating, in the most explicit manner, the data upon which the estimate is based ; and that it is most desirable that estimates should be illustrated by drawings.

2. That as the term "**Ore in Sight**" is frequently used to indicate two separate factors in an estimate, namely :

   (*a*) **Ore Blocked Out**—that is Ore exposed on at least three sides within reasonable distance of each other—and

   (*b*) **Ore which may be reasonably assumed to exist** though not actually "blocked out,"

these two factors should in all cases be kept distinct, as (*a*) is governed by fixed rules, whilst (*b*) is dependent upon individual judgment and local experience.

3. That in making use of the term "Ore in Sight" an Engineer should demonstrate that the Ore so denominated is capable of being profitably extracted under the working conditions obtaining in the district.

4. That the Members of the Institution be urged to protect the best interests of the Profession by using their influence in every way possible to prevent and discourage the use of the term "Ore in Sight" except as defined above ; and the Council also strongly advise that no ambiguity or mystery in this connection should be tolerated, as they (the Council) consider that such ambiguity is an indication of dishonesty or incompetency.

By Order of the Council,

C. McDERMID,

Secretary

SALISBURY HOUSE, LONDON, E.C.,
September 30th. 1902.

STAFF ARRANGEMENTS

DIAGRAM OF EXPENDITURE AND RESULTS,

SHEWING THE RELATION BETWEEN THE TECHNICAL DEPARTMENTS AS REGARDS RESULTS
AND THE BUSINESS STAFF AS REGARDS EXPENDITURE IN THE GENERAL ORGANIZATION

The GENERAL MANAGER, as illustrated in the diagram opposite, controls the expenditure on the one hand, generally indicated by blue lines, and through the Assayer, the extraction of Gold on the other hand generally indicated by red lines

The COMMERCIAL SUPERINTENDENT or MINES SECRETARY specially controls the expenditure by checking the outgoing of Wages and Stores to the various departmental accounts   This he does through the Wages and Stores Clerks   Where the amount is carried to Development or Erection of New Works Account, the thin black lines indicate this check , the thin blue lines where carried to Working Account

The Assayer tests the efficiency of the process by taking check assays at the various points of the operation   The thin red lines indicate this check

The ACCOUNTANT deals with the Accounts and Book-keeping Records of Expenditure as furnished to him by the Wages and Stores Clerks

The EXPENDITURE on account of WORKING the Mines and Gold extraction processes is carried to the various departments in thick blue lines

The EXPENDITURE on account of DEVELOPMENT OF THE MINE or of ERECTION OF NEW WORKS is carried to those accounts in thick black lines

The VARIOUS DEPARTMENTS of Mining, Milling, and Cyaniding are managed by the various Superintendents as indicated, and the results of their technical work, being shewn in the departmental Reports, consist briefly of the mining the ore and the extraction of Gold from it

LOSS IN PROCESS AND LOSS IN TAILINGS OR RESIDUES, refer to that portion of the Gold which has not been saved in the process   A specimen of the loss will be found in the Gold Statement on page 181   One of the great aims of the Technical Departments should be to minimize this loss

Economical working in general will largely depend upon harmonious co-operation between the Departmental Managers on the one hand, and the Commercial Superintendent or Mines Secretary on the other

It will be observed that, under the control of the General Manager, the General Expenditure Sheet (No 8) is left in the hands of the Commercial Superintendent or Mines Secretary, and he must account for the expenditure distributed to the different departments according to the lines laid down in this book, generally indicated by the blue and black lines and figures in the diagram   He also will receive and credit the Gold in like manner in the Gold Account or Statement, indicated in red lines in the diagram

By way of example, the cost per ton of treating an Ore is shewn in the diagram under the heading of Expenditure Sheet, and the fine Gold produced calculated in sterling, is shewn in the Gold Account or Statement , a balance is struck between the two, which leaves an apparent profit of 8/6 per ton

The details of the purchases and the distribution of the Stores, and the allocation of Wages, might also have been shewn in a diagramatic form, but with the diagram opposite as a specimen, this can easily be done if desired

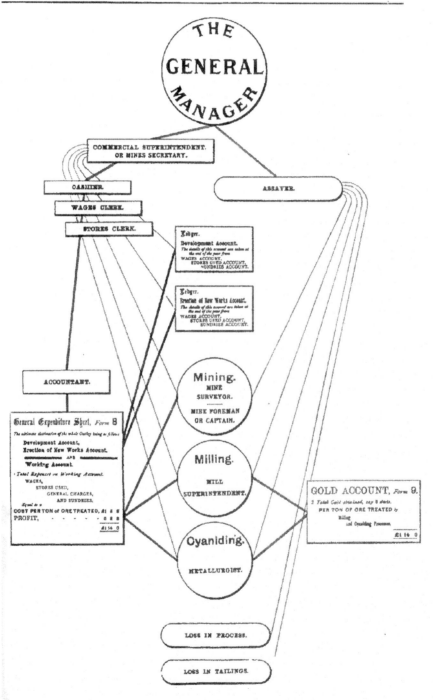

RULES AND SPECIMENS

OF

THE DEPARTMENTAL REPORTS OR RECORDS.

Introduction.

THE general Staff Arrangements having been set out in the previous pages, it is now proposed to deal with their application to the Departments.

It will be observed in the following specimen set of Reports that rules to guide the responsible officer of the department in making his report precede the specimens, most of which have been filled in by way of example. It is intended that these rules should be inserted at the beginning of each book used, so as to be constantly before the officers for their direction. Many of the rules are the same in one department as in another, but it is better that the instructions for each several department should be set out in full, so that they may be available for the officer of each department without reference to the rules of any other.

The Forms **A** to **E** have reference to clearly defined working departments, but the Form **F** is for Power which has to be distributed among the other departments which use it. Form **G** is for Repairs of Plant, where a specially equipped Maintenance Department exists, and the costs have to be distributed, so that the repairs of each department are shewn separately.

The Departmental or Technical Reports, which are the equivalent of the Log Books kept by Ships' Officers and Engineers at sea, should shew the work done by the department, the cost of which is finally charged to that department in the General Expenditure Sheet (No. **8**), under the headings of Cash and Stores.

These Departmental Reports should be made outside of the Counting-House, and as far as possible on the ground where the work is carried on. Where one department has work carried on at widely separated points, a separate record should be kept at each.

The specimens of the Departmental Reports shewn have been taken from different mines and from various localities, and are therefore to be looked at simply as examples of the method of filling in; and no scientific or practical deduction as to methods of working should be drawn from the circumstances and limited figures therein given. This book is not written with the purpose of shewing how the work should be done, but of shewing how the work done should be recorded, and of shewing how the expenditure may be checked by proper accounts, and the processes by the sampling and assaying.

The diagram given on page 40 shews the tests made of the Gold in the different departments, and the results collected together in the Gold Statement (No. **9**).

The Specimen Forms submitted include most of the general forms required. Some, such as for Surface Prospecting, are only applicable and useful to Companies with extensive . . . . where deep-lying in . . . .

Surface Prospecting.

Form **A.**

Responsible Officer.—The Mine Surveyor or the Prospector.

Definition of Work covered by this Report.

SURFACE PROSPECTING will include only that general survey of the locality, accompanied by costeening, tracing and sampling outcrops, sinking shallow trial pits, and such like work, which usually precede the actual testing of definite points by underground prospecting.

This Form is designedly left as a sheet of blank paper, because the earlier stages of work will be difficult to tabulate. The first business of a Prospector is to find the position of the reef, and it is this and other collateral information which is sought for in this report.

Entries for this Book.

These should come from the Prospector's Note Book and the Foreman's Order Book carried by the Prospector.

Entries in this Book should shew the following :—

The total number of men, though not the cash amount, employed during the month by this department.

This should be compared with the number of men charged in the Wages Sheet to this department.

The quantity of important Stores used, though not the cash amount.

This should be compared with the quantity of important Stores Charged to this department in the Stores Used Sheet.

Amount of work done which is charged for in the Expenditure Sheet, under the head of **Prospecting**—*Surface.*

Samples.

Suggestions as to sampling surface exposures are given at page 29. The prospector should mention in his reports all mineralogical specimens brought into the office for identification, or samples taken for assaying, and the place whence these are taken.

Specimen.

See pages 45 and 46.

Copies for the Head Office.

A copy of the Surface Prospecting Report Book to be forwarded monthly to the Head Office on the Form provided for the purpose.

FOR GOLD MINING BUSINESS.

SPACE RESERVED FOR MS. NOTES.

WORK DONE *for the Month of*

...*190*   .

Date. ....

Inspector,
(or Mine Surveyor.)

Underground Prospecting.

The following Forms are provided for the different divisions of work :—

FORM Ba.—*FOR TRIAL ADITS, SHAFTS, WINZES, CROSSCUTS, &c.*
   ,,   Bb.—*FOR DIAMOND DRILL BORING.*

THE REPORT BOOK FOR TRIAL ADITS, SHAFTS, WINZES, CROSSCUTS, &c.

Form Ba.

The rules for keeping Form Ba are almost identical with those in Form O (see page 53), the Responsible Officer being the Mine Surveyor. For specimen, see pages 49 and 50.

Definition of Work covered by this Report.

UNDERGROUND PROSPECTING will include boring (which will generally be placed under a sub-head of its own), sinking trial shafts, driving trial crosscuts and trial levels, trial adits, and so forth, as distinguished from permanent shafts, levels, &c., intended subsequently to be used in actual mining.

As some work done for prospecting purposes may ultimately be utilized for the later stages, it may not always be easy to divide this head from development. In some cases the most convenient demarcation may be a time limit,—that is, all work not clearly coming under permanent development up to a certain date may be classified under the present head ; and all work done after the fixed date, when the trial stage may be considered over and the Mine proved in that section or part, may be classed as development.

Amount of work done is charged for in the Expenditure Sheet (No. **8**), under the head of **Prospecting—***Underground.*

The following are the rules for keeping

THE REPORT BOOK FOR DIAMOND DRILL BORING :—

Form Bb.

Responsible Officer.—Mine Surveyor, but Form **Bb** is to be written up by the Diamond Drilling Foreman.

Entries for this Book.

The entries of work done should be made in this book direct when the facts are ascertained. They should not be filtered through another book and then written clean into this book, as such a course is apt to create errors, and would only entail unnecessary work.

Entries in this Book should shew the following :—

The total number of men employed during the month by this department, though not the cash amount of their Wages.

This should be compared with the number of men charged in the Wages Sheet to this department.

The quantity of important Stores used, though not the cash amount, as indicated below :—

    SPARE BORING RODS.
    CROWNS.
    DIAMONDS.
    ANY OTHER IMPORTANT STORES.

These pass through the Store Accounts, in common with all other Stores. These items, however, are of so much importance to the Diamond Drill Boring Department, that the Foreman should always be cognizant of what is being consumed and what is on hand.

Amount of work done, which is charged for in the Expenditure Sheet (No. 8), under the head of **Prospecting**—*Underground.*

Samples of Ore.

Samples of every description of rock passed through should be sent to the Assay Office for mineralogical identification or for assaying, and the point at which these samples are taken should be recorded in the column provided for the purpose.

The core should be carefully preserved, numbered and registered.

Specimen.

Form **Bb.**—A specimen of Diamond Drill Boring Form is given on pages 51 and 52.

Copies for the Head Office.

A copy of the Diamond Drill Boring Report book to be forwarded monthly to the Head Office on the Form provided for the purpose.

....*Mine.*   WORK DONE *for the*

Number of Men Employed.		Number of Shaft.	No. of Drive.	DISTANCE DRIVEN OR SUNK.		Direction.	Formation.	Dip.	Thick of Rfel
NATIVES.	OTHERS.			During Month.	Total to Date.				

Month of ....

Output. Tons.	Assay Value per Ton.	Pannings.	REMARKS.

Date

Mine Surveyor.

H

WORK DONE *for the*

Number of Men Employed.	No. of Hours Boring.	Date.		Depth Bored.		Total Depth.		Core obtained.		Nature of Strata.
TIVES. OTHERS.				Ft.	In.	Ft.	In.	Ft.	In.	
		Brought forward,				40	5			
		June,	8	2	10	43	3	2	0	Chert, jointy & broken.
		,,	9	2	8	45	11	2	4	Shale, very jointy.
				2	7	48	6	2	6	Blue Limestone.
		,,	10	1	2	49	8	1	2	Ditto.
				3	7	53	3			Blue Slate.
		,,	11	5	0	58	3			Ditto.
		,,	12	3	10	62	1	7	6	Ditto.
		,,	13			62	1			
				etc.,		etc.				

Month of June, 1896.

Size of Crown in use.	REMARKS.	Sample Taken.
8"	Boiler steamed badly to-day.	
	Ground still very jointy, and bores slowly.	
	Lost the core in drawing; made spring ready.	
	Put down, but could only get over 1' of the core.	
	Had trouble to get over the core. Bored 5 feet, and in drawing lost the core again.	
	Did not get down over the core until 2.30 p.m. Bored 3 ft. 10 in.; drew, and got 7 ft. 6 in. of core.	
	Took slide valve out of engine, and altered the cut-off. Fixed water pipe from pump to feed barrel.	

Date,...................................

....Diamond Driller.

Date,.... ....

..   Mine Surveyor

Mining and Ore Transport.

Form **C.**

Responsible Officers.

This book is to be written up by the Mine Surveyor or his Assistant.

Definition of Work covered by this Report.

DEVELOPMENT will include all work intended for permanent use in the mining of ore, such as winding, pumping, and ventilating shafts, main adits, levels, drives, winzes, and crosscuts, designed for the blocking out, stoping, and conveyance of ore to the surface.

It will usually be convenient to keep "Shafts" as a separate sub-head of this heading.

MINING will include principally the stoping of ore, timbering, filling stopes with waste, underground sorting ; and also the execution of any drives, crosscuts, winzes, upraises, &c., necessary for stoping purposes, and not included in the previously completed development. It will also include the tramming of ore to the foot of winding shaft or to the exit of adits, when not carried on by mechanical appliances.

UNDERGROUND TRANSPORT.—This head will include the cost of haulage, by mechanical means, from the loading of ore into trucks to its delivery at the foot of shaft or at the mouth of adit, as the case may be.

SORTING.—Surface Sorting is usually done at the Shaft head, and may therefore be conveniently reported on this form.

MECHANICAL HAULAGE AND TRANSPORT are dealt with under Power Forms **F.**

TRANSPORT TO MILL will include the cost of conveyance of ore from bins or dumps at pit head or adit mouth, or in trucks direct from same to the ore bins at the mill.

Entries for this Book.

The entries should be made in this book, as far as possible, when the facts are ascertained. They should not be filtered through another book and then written clean into this book, as such a course is apt to create errors, and would certainly create useless work.

In large works, in the case of the Foremen of the different parts of the work contributing to the information, it may be necessary to take such information from the Foremen's Note Books under the full heads, in a systematic manner, and the responsible officer should at once write it into this book.

Entries in this book should shew the following :—

The total number of men employed during the month by this department, though not the cash amount of their wages. The number of men should be shewn as employed in the different sections and levels of the Mine in *Sinking, Driving, Stoping, &c.*

This should be compared with the number of men charged in the Wages Sheet to this department.

The quantity of important Stores Used, though not the cash amount, as indicated below :—

DYNAMITE.
DRILL STEEL.
ANY OTHER IMPORTANT STORES.

FOR GOLD MINING BUSINESS.

The amount of work which is charged for in the Expenditure Sheet (No. **8**), page 149 under the following heads :—

Development—
    Sinking.
    Driving Levels.

Mining—
    Sinking.
    Driving Levels.
    Stoping.
    Tramming and Haulage to Surface.

Transport to Mill—

Renewals or Repairs.

Notes to be made in the Remarks column of any repairs which have been made during the month that have not been reported on Form **G**, so that in the Expenditure Sheet they may be charged to—

MAINTENANCE OF PLANT.

Mining—
    Pumping Gear.
    Rock Drills and Compressors.

Haulage—
    Hauling Gear.
    Underground Tramway.
    Main Shaft.
    Houses over Hauling Engines.

Transport—
    Maintenance of Tramways.

Stock of Ore to be checked Monthly by this Book.

The following is a sketch of the way the Stock should be written into the Remarks column every month :—

Stock of Ore brought forward from last month, ... tons.
Output of Ore mined during this month, ... ,,

Ore delivered to Mill or Dry Crushers during month, ... ,,

Stock of Ore at Mine carried forward to next month, ... ,,

Note.—*The above stock should remain in the Books at the Credit of the Working Account until it is delivered for treatment.*

Reserves of Ore.

Notes should also be made, from time to time, giving estimate of amount of Ore in sight. At end of each financial year the Reserves should be carefully measured up and certified by a competent Surveyor.

Samples of Ore.

Samples of all ore mined are to be sent to the Assay Office daily, weekly, or monthly, as arranged. For suggestions as to method of taking samples, see page 34. It should be clearly stated whether the samples are taken from the working faces or from the ore brought to grass.

Specimens.

See pages 55 and 56 ; also alternative forms **Ca** and **Cb**, see pages 57 to 60.

Copies for the Head Office.

A copy of the Mining Report Book to be forwarded monthly to the Head Office on the Form provided for the purpose.

.... *Mine.*   WORK DONE *for the Month of*

Number of Men Employed.		Number of Shaft.	No. of Drives.	DISTANCE DRIVEN.		Direction.	Formation.	Dip.	Thickness of Reef.	
ATIVES.	OTHERS.			During Month.	Total to Date.					
			MINING.	Feet.	Feet.				Inches.	
			Drive No. 4	54	700	S. W.	Limestone	7° West	35	
			„ C.c. to left at 355'	31	68	S.E.	„	„	16	
			„ „ 407'	23	46	„	„	„	15	
			„ „ 454'	9	33	„	„	„	15	
19	4		No. 16	43	533	S. W.	„	„	28	1
			No. 16a	19	266	N.E.	„	„	27	
			No. 4a	57	328	„	„	„	15	
			Slope off 4a	36	46	S. W.	„	„	18	
			No. 13a	43	124	N.E.	„	„	6	

STOPING.

    Here follow the details of Stoping, giving numbers o

TRAMMING AND HAULAGE TO SURFACE.

    Here follow the details of Tramming, giving number

SORTING.

    Here follow the details of Surface Sorting, if any

TRANSPORT TO MILL.

    Here follow the details of Transport to Mill, giving

....*18*

...ay ...at ...on.	Panning.	REMARKS.
		Double shift. Holed through on Drive No. 4a.
...an. ...0		*Double shift. Through on 1ba.*
		Do. Do. 1b.
		Inferior reef.

...pes worked, number of men employed, and tons extracted.

...men employed and tons of ore dealt with.

...mber of men employed and tons of ore transported to Mill.

𝕹ote.

This example is taken from workings in an approximately horizontal seam, such as is worked in some districts in the Transvaal. Where sinking is carried on an additional column headed "Feet Sunk" can be added; or the Forms **Ca** or **Cb** can be used.

Date,..................................

....*Mine Surveyor.*

.... *Mine.*   WORK DONE *for th*

Lease No. and Name of Reef.	SHAFTS SUNK.				WINZES SUNK.				LEVELS DRIVEN.			
	No. of Men Employed.	Nos.	During Fortnight.	Total Depth.	No. of Men Employed	Nos.	During Fortnight.	Total Depth.	Nos. Name, and Position.	No. of Men Employed.	During Fortnight	Total Len
			Ft. Ins.	Ft. Ins.			Ft. Ins.	Ft. Ins.			Ft. Ins. Ft. Ins.	Ft. Ins.

Month of ..

	STOPES ON REEFS.					CROSSCUTS DRIVEN.						REMARKS.
	Position.	No. of Men Employed	Width of Reef.	Quality.	Output.	Position.	No. of Men Employed	During Fortnight.		Total Length.		
			Ft. In.		Tons.			Ft. In.	Ft. In.	Ft. In.	Ft. In.	

58

....*Mine.*

MINING.

WORK DONE *for the*

Nos.		Shifts.	Distance for Month.	Total Distance.	Thickness of Reef.	Value of Reef.	Nos. of Stopes.	Shifts.	Thickness of Reef.	Value of Reef.	Output.	REMARKS.
Crosscuts.	Drives.		Feet.	Feet.	Ft. dec.	Dwt. dec.			Ft. dec.	Dwt. dec.	Tons	
	DRIVING.							STOPING.				

Month of ....

DEVELOPING.

		SINKING.					DRIVING.						REMARKS.
	Shifts.	Distance for Month.	Total Distance.	Thickness of Reef.	Value of Reef.	Nos.		Shifts.	Distance for Month.	Total Distance.	Thickness of Reef.	Value of Reef.	
Weeks.		Feet.	Feet.	Ft. dec.	Dwt. dec.	Cross-cuts.	Drives.		Feet.	Feet.	Ft. dec.	Dwt. dec.	

Milling and Crushing.

Form D.

Responsible Officer.

This book is to be written up by the Mill Superintendent.

Definition of Work covered by this Report.

MILLING AND CRUSHING will include the treatment of the ore from the time it leaves the ore bins above the mills to the time the tailings leave the mill, or the crushed ore (in direct cyaniding) leaves the dry crushers, also retorting amalgam.

A separate Form of same pattern may be used for Milling and one for Crushing.

Entries for this Book.

The entries should be made in this book, day by day, when the facts are ascertained. They should not be filtered through another book, and then written clean into this book, as such a course is apt to create errors, and would certainly create useless work.

In large works where the Foremen of the different parts of the work contribute to the information, it may be necessary to take such information from the Foremen's Note Books, under the full heads, in a systematic manner, and the responsible officer should write it at once into this book.

Entries in this Book should shew the following :—

The total number of men, though not the cash amount, employed during the month by this department.

This should be compared with the number of men charged in the Wages Sheet to this department.

The quantity of important Stores used, though not the cash amount, as indicated below : —

> Mercury.
>
> Spare Parts of Mill.
>
> Shoes.
>
> Dies.
>
> Driving Belts.
>
> Any other important Stores.

The amount of work done which is charged for in the Expenditure Sheet (No. 8), page 149, under the head of Milling and Crushing.

Renewals and Repairs.

Notes to be made in the Remarks column of any repairs which have been made during the month that have not been reported on form G, so that in the Expenditure Sheet they may be charged to—

MAINTENANCE OF PLANT.

Mills, Rock-breakers, &c.

Houses over Mills.

Mill Stock of Ore to be checked monthly by this book.

The following is a sketch of the way the Stock should be written into the Remarks column every month :—

Stock of Ore in Bin, brought forward from last month,   tons.

Ore received from Mine during this month, ...   ,,

Ore Milled or Crushed during this month, ...   ,,

NOTE.—*This is the figure taken for the Gold Statement, No.* **9.**

Stock of Ore in Bin, carried forward to next month,   ...   ,,

NOTE.—*The above Stock, together with the Stock of Ore at the Mine, remains in the Books at the Credit of Working Account until it is delivered for treatment.*

Samples to be taken by Assayer.

Samples of all Ore filled into the Mill should be taken by the Assayer daily, weekly, or monthly, as may be arranged by the management (see page 34).

Specimen.

See pages 63 and 64.

Copies for the Head Office.

A copy of the Milling and Crushing Report Book or Books (if kept separate) should be forwarded monthly to the Head Office on the Forms provided for the purpose.

WORK DONE *for th*

Number of Men Employed.		DATE.		Number of Stamps Running.	TIME.		DROP OF STAMPS.		CAUSE OF STOPPAGE.
NATIVES.	OTHERS.				Hours Working.	Hours Stopped.	Height.	No. per Min.	
		Dec.	1	5	24				
			2	,,	24				
			3	,,	24				
			4	10	24				
			5	,,	19	5			Repairing Driving Belt.
			7	,,	24				
			8	5	24				
			9	10	24				

Month of December, 1895.

	NAME OF ORE MILLED.				*Filling Assay.*	*Weight of Amalgam.*	*Concentrates.*	*REMARKS.*
	Stope No. 2.	*Stope No. 3.*	*Stope No. 9.*	*Stope No. 10.*				
ons.	*Tons.*							
	9							
	7							
	8							
	16							
	6							
	15							
	8							
	22							
	91	= 165 *tons.*				3600 028.		

Note.

The screen used and height of discharge should be noted once on each sheet, and any change in same should be recorded under "Remarks."

The "Filling" Assays may or may not be given in this sheet. These can be obtained from the Assay Certificate Book.

Any change in the arrangement of the amalgamating tables, blankets, &c., should be carefully recorded under "Remarks."

Where Concentrates bulk largely, a separate Form may be necessary for recording their treatment. For Dry Crushing the headings of the Columns can be suitably altered.

Date........

Mine Superintendent.

Cyaniding.

Form **E.**

Responsible Officer.

This book is to be written up by the Metallurgist who has charge of the Extraction Process.

Definition of work covered by this Report.

CYANIDING will include the cost of transporting Tailings from the mill to the vats, or where direct Cyaniding is employed, the transport of the Crushed Ore from the screens to the vats, the treatment there, the recovery of the bullion in bars, and the discharge of residues to the dumps.

TREATMENT OF SLIMES will include (where employed) preparation and conveyance of slimes from the slime pits to the vats, treatment there, recovery of bullion, and discharge of the spent slimes.

Entries for this Book.

The entries should be made in this book when the facts are ascertained. They should not be filtered through another book, and then written clean into this book, as such a course is apt to create errors, and would certainly create useless work.

In large works, in the case of the Foreman of the different parts of the work contributing to the information, it may be necessary to take the information from the Foreman's Note Books, under full heads, in a systematic manner, and the responsible officer should write it at once into this book.

Entries in this Book should shew the following :—

The total number of men, though not the cash amount, employed during the month by this department.

This should be compared with the number of men charged in the Wages Sheet to this department.

The quantity of important Stores used, though not the cash amount, such as—

CYANIDE.

ZINC FOR PRECIPITATION.

ANY OTHER IMPORTANT STORES.

The amount of work which is charged for in the Expenditure Sheet under the heading of **Cyaniding**.

Renewals or Repairs.

Notes to be made in the Remarks column of any repairs which have been made during the month, so that the expenditure charges under the following heads will be approximately explained thereby :—

MAINTENANCE OF PLANT.

Cyanide Plant.

Houses over Cyanide Plant.

Stock of Tailings to be checked monthly by this book.

In the event of Tailings being carried over from one month to another, a jotting of same should be given in the space reserved on the left-hand side every month, as follows :—

Stock of Tailings brought forward from last month, ... tons
Tailings received from Battery during this month, ... ,,

Tailings charged into Vats during this month, ... ,,

Stock of Tailings carried forward to next month, ... ,,

Stock of Slimes to be treated in the same way.

CONCENTRATES.

No special form has been provided for the treatment of concentrates, but a suitable form should be used for any process adopted.

Samples to be sent to Assay Office.

Samples of all Ore filled into vats, also of the residues and sump solutions, to be sent to the Assay Office daily, or as arranged.

Specimens.

For Sands treatment, see pages 67 and 68. For alternative form, see pages 69 and 70.

For Slimes treatment, see pages 71 and 72.

The figures relating to the monthly clean-up may in some cases be more conveniently reported on a separate form.

Copies for the Head Office.

A copy of the Cyanide Report Book to be forwarded monthly to the Head Office on the Form provided for the purpose.

WORK DONE *for the Month of*

DATE.		No. of Tank.	Gross Weight.	MOISTURE.		Net Dry Weight.	ASSAY VALUE.				APPARENT EXTRACTION	
							Tailings or Ore.		Residue.			
Charged	Discharged.			%	Weight.		P. Ton.	Contents.	P. Ton.	Contents.	P. Ton.	Weight
			Tons.		Tons.	Tons.	Dwts. Grns.	Ounces.	Dwts. Grns.	Ounces.	Dwts. Grns.	Ounces.

189

ACTUAL PRODUCTION.				PARTICULARS OF BULLION.			STRENGTH OF SOLUTION.	CYANIDE CONSUMED.	ASSAY OF SUMP SOLUTIONS.	NUMBER OF MEN EMPLOYED	REMARKS.
Weight, of Gold.	% of Contents.	P. Ton.	Nos. of Bars.	Weight.	Fineness.	Weight, Fine Gold.					
ounces.		Oz. Dwts. Grns.		Ounces.		Ounces.			Lbs.		

Date.

Metallurgist.

...................................Mine.   WORK DONE *for the*

SUMMARY.

Number of Men employed—   Whites..............   Natives..............

Tons treated in Vats (Dry Weight), ...

Tons included in Clean-up (Dry Weight), ...

Average Assay of Tailings treated, ...

Average Assay of Spent Tailings, ...

Percentage of Gold extracted, as shewn by assays of Tailings treated and Spent Tailings,

Estimated yield, in ounces, calculated from ditto, ...

Percentage of Gold actually recovered, ...

Bullion recovered, ounces, ...

Fineness of Bullion, ...

— Fine Gold, ounces, ...

Gold in Solution, ...

Consumption of Cyanide per ton of Tailings treated, ...

Ditto.,   total weight for Month, ...

Samps on last day of Month, ...

KCy + NaHO, ...

Strong = ...

Weak = ...

Wash = ...

Assay Values of Samps on last day of Month, ...

Strong   ...   .

Weak   ...   .

Wash   ...   .

FOR GOLD MINING BUSINESS.

Month of 190

Charge No.	WEIGHT.			DATE OF		ASSAY OF						EXTRACTION.		
	Gross Tons.	Moisture %	Dry Tons.	Charge.	Discharge.	Ore or Tailings Treated.			Spent Ore, or Tailings.					
						Ozs.	Dwts.	Grs.	Ozs.	Dwts.	Grs.	Ozs.	Dwts.	Grs.

WORK DONE *for the Month of*

DATE	No. of Charge.	No. of Agitator.	Time Agitated.	Weight of Charge.		Strength of Solution in Agitators	ASSAY VALUES (on Dry Weight).			EXTRACTION.				GOLD REC
				Total Weight	Dry Weight		Charged Slimes.	Pressed (or Settled) Residues.	Washed Press (or Settled) Residues.	Calculated.		Actual.	Bullion	Fine O
			Hours.	Tons.	Tons.	%	Dwts. Grns.	Grns.	Grns.	Dwts. Grns.	%	%	Total Ounces.	Total Ou
1	2	3	4	5	6	7	8	9	10	11	12	13	14	15

190

ED.	Amount of Weak Sump Wash used.	Amount of Water Wash used.	K'Cy Test of Sump.		Assay of Sump.		REMARKS.
			Strong.	Weak.	Strong.	Weak.	
Grns	Tons.	Tons.	%	%	Grains per Ton.	Grains per Ton.	
16	17	18	19	20	21	22	

Notes.

5. Total Weight of Dry Slimes plus Water plus Solution in Agitator.
6. Dry Weight of Slimes calculated in Column 5.
10. This will be determined occasionally to check the washing in the presses (or by Decantation).
13.
14.
15. Made up from the actual gold recovered in the clean up, the figures appearing once a month or as often as the clean up takes place.
16.
19.
20. Will probably be taken daily.
21.
22. Will probably be taken weekly.

Where Silver is present in sufficient quantity, Columns 8, 9, 10, 11, 12, 13, 15, and 16 will require to be duplicated.

Decimals of dwts. may be substituted for grains.

KCy+NaHO Test of Sumps, { Strong............... / Weak...............

Cyanide—Total Weight consumed,...............lbs.

Cyanide consumed per ton,...............lbs.

Cloth used,...............yds.

Loss of Gold in Smelting,...............

No. of Men employed—Whites,...............

       ,,   ,, Natives,...............

Date.

.... *Metallurgist.*

Power.

The following Forms are provided for the different divisions of power :—

FORM Fa.—*STEAM POWER.*
    ,,   **Fb.**—*TRANSMISSION OF ELECTRICAL POWER.*
    ,,   **Fc.**—*OIL ENGINES.*

No Form is provided for water power, but monthly report should be sent when water power is used. Such report should give information as to the supply of water in the head dam, the rainfall during month, and any other point that influences the power available from this source.

POWER REPORT FOR STEAM.

Form **Fa.**

The design of this Monthly Report is to shew that the **Consumption of Fuel** is kept down to its lowest limit, the most work got out of the **Engine,** and that proper attention has been given by those in charge.

Responsible Officer.—The Mechanical Engineer.

Definition of Work covered by this Report.

MOTIVE POWER will include the distribution of steam power, from the point of generation to the point of application, and will usually be subdivided to the several heads chargeable, as under :—

MINING.

    Rock Drills.
    Underground Transport or Tramming.
    Haulage to Surface.
    Pumping.

MILLING.

CYANIDING.

    Sands.
    Slimes.

Entries for this Book.

The Engine Attendant should, every hour, note the particulars required on a slate or board, and the daily summations or averages of these figures should be taken by the Mechanical Engineer and entered in this book.

The daily consumption of fuel should be carefully estimated where it cannot be weighed.

The Engineer should make a special test, say every three months, of the efficiency of the engines and boilers, working out the consumption per indicated horse-power of the engines, and the water evaporated per pound of fuel in the boilers ; and space in the Report is provided for these figures.

Entries in this Book should shew the following :—

The total number of men, though not the cash amount, employed directly in working for the following departments :—

> *Pumping.*
> *Haulage.*
> *Transport to Mill.*
> *Milling.*
> *Any other Department requiring Power.*

The quantity of important Stores used, but not the cash amount, as indicated below :—

> OIL.
> SPARE PARTS.
> ANY OTHER STORES.

The fuel passes through the Stores Accounts, in common with all other Stores. The Engineer in charge, however, should always be cognizant of what is consumed and what is on hand.

The Fuel Account, especially, should always be checked in its total debits by the Accountant by reference to this sheet.

Stock of Fuel at the Engine-house should be jotted in the Remarks column monthly, as follows :—

Stock of Fuel brought forward from last month, ... tons.
Quantity added to stock during this month, ... ,,
,,

Total available, ... ,,

Fuel consumed during this month. ... ... ,,

Stock of Fuel carried forward to next month, ... ,,

Distribution of Power.

If the power should be distributed between the Pumping. Hauling, and the Mill, or other department, the distribution should be ascertained as nearly as possible, and instructions given accordingly to the Wages Clerk and Stores Clerk, so that they can observe the proper allocation of wages and stores, throughout the year, to the proper departments.

Renewals or Repairs.

Notes to be made in the Remarks column of any repairs which have been made during the month that have not been reported on Form **G,** so that in the Expenditure Sheet (No. **8**) they may be charged to—

MAINTENANCE OF PLANT.

> *Pumping Engines and Boilers.*
> *Hauling Engines and Boilers.*
> *Mill Engines and Boilers.*

Specimen.

A specimen of the Form is filled up on pages 75 and 76.

Copies for the Head Office.

A copy of the Power Report Book **Fa** to be forwarded monthly to the Head Office on the Form provided for the purpose, separate sheets being used for each engine where more than one are in use. Each engine should have a distinguishing number or name.

WORK DONE *for the*

ENGINE No.	Particulars of ENGINE.	Particulars of BOILERS.
	Diameter of H.-P. Cylinder = 15".	No. 1.—Lancashire, 7' 6" x 30' 6".
Driving Stamp Mill, Crushers, & Air Compressors.	Diameter of L.-P. Cylinder = 30".	No. 2.— Do., 7' 6" x 30' 6".
	Length of Stroke = 42".	No. 3.—Cornish, 6' 0" x 24' 0".
	Condensing (Jet)	

Date.		Time Run. Hours.	Revolutions Daily, Number, by Counter.	Grade Expansion. Cut-off.	Approximate Indicated H.-P.	Boilers Used. Nos.	Fuel Used. Lbs.	Steam Pressure. Lbs.	Water Used. Galls
May	1	24	115,210	¼		1 and 2	12,200	80	
„	2	22	104,200	¼		1 „ 2	11,000	80	
„	3	24	113,214	¼		2 „ 3	12,300	80	
„	4	24	114,300	¼		2 „ 3	12,200	80	

FOR GOLD MINING BUSINESS.

Month of May, 1896.

FUEL.	**WATER.**

Amount of Fuel used in lbs. per Indicated H.-P. per hour.

$$\frac{Fuel\ used\ per\ hour}{I.H.-P.} = \quad lbs.\ Fuel\ per\ H.-P.\ per\ hour.$$

Amount of Water evaporated in lbs. per pound of Fuel used,

$$\frac{Gallons\ Water \times 10\ lbs.}{lbs.\ Fuel.} = \quad lbs.\ Water\ per\ 1\ lb.\ Fuel.$$

GENERAL REMARKS.

Crank-pin heated—stopped for 2 hours.

No. 1 Boiler thrown off for examination.

Coal small and wet.

Date,...................................

..Mechanical Engineer.

POWER REPORT BOOK—ELECTRICAL TRANSMISSION.

Form **F**b.

Responsible Officer.—The Electrical Engineer.

Definition of Work covered by this Report.

MOTIVE POWER, as set out here, will include the electrical distribution from the point of generation to the point of application, and will usually be subdivided to the several heads as enumerated under Motive Power on page 73.

Entries for this Book.

In case of the Foremen of the different parts of the work contributing to the information, it may be necessary to take such information from the Foremen's Note Books under the full heads. When this course is followed, it should be systematically done, and the Responsible Officer should write it at once into this book.

Entries in this Book should shew:—

The total number of men employed in working the following departments :—

> *Haulage.*
> *Transport.*
> *Milling.*
> *Cyaniding.*
> *Electro-depositing.*
> *Electric Lighting.*
> *Other Departments requiring Electrical Power.*

The particulars of repairs should form the items charged to the General Expenditure Sheet (No. **8**.)

The quantity of important Stores used, but not the cash amount, as indicated below :—

> SPARE PARTS.
> LINESMAN'S STORES.
> RUNNING STORES—OILS, BELTS, AND ROPES.
> OTHER STORES.

These pass through the Store Accounts in common with all other Stores. These items, however, are of so much importance to the Electrical Department, that the Foreman should always be cognizant of what is being consumed and what is on hand.

Renewals or Repairs.

Notes to be made in the Remarks column of any repairs which have been made during the month which have not been reported on Form **G**, so that in the Expenditure Sheet they may be charged to—

MAINTENANCE OF PLANT.

Dynamos, Motors, and Transformers.
Cable Lines.
Switchboard and Instruments.

77

Specimen.

See pages 79 and 80.

Copies for the Head Office.

A copy of the Power Report Book **Fb** to be forwarded monthly to the Head Office on the Form provided for the purpose.

WORK DONE *for the*

GENERATORS.

DATE.	Hours Run.	Speed.	Volts	Amperes.	REMARKS.	
Monday, May 1	24	615	610	43·5	Cool and Sparkless.	
Tuesday, „ 2	24	640	610	40·0	Do.	
Wednes., „ 3	24	639	605	49·5	Do.	10 minutes' stoppage to change early
Thursday, „ 4	22	630	605	50·0	Do.	2 hours' stoppage on account of she race choked with debris.
Friday, „ 5	24	630	605	44·0	Do.	
Saturday, „ 6	12	625	605	50·0	Do.	

Month of May, 1896.

MOTORS.

DATE.		Hours Run.	Speed.	Volts.	Amperes.	Load.	REMARKS.
May	1	24	765	570	45·0	15 stamps	Cool and Sparkless.
„	2	24	765	560	47·5	20 „	Do.
„	3	24	760	555	49·0	20 „	Do.
„	4	22	760	555	49·0	20 „	Do.
„	5	24	777	580	43·5	15 „	Sparking slightly and cool.
„	6	12	750	540	50·5	20 „	Sparking and hot.

The Motor ran 130 hours = 118 hours of 20 stamp capacity.

Date,...

Electrical Engineer.

POWER REPORT BOOK—OIL ENGINE.

Form **F**c.

This Monthly Report is to shew that the efficiency of the Engine is being maintained, and that the most work is being got out of it for the minimum amount of oil used.

Responsible Officer.—The Mechanical Engineer.

Definition of Work covered by this Report.

MOTIVE POWER, as set out here, will include the distribution of Power from the point of generation to the point of application, and will usually be subdivided to the several heads as enumerated under Motive Power on page 73.

Entries for this Book.

A log should be kept on a slate or black board by the Engine Attendant, and the daily totals transferred to this book.

Entries in this Book should shew the following :—

The total number of men employed directly in working for the various departments :—

> *Haulage.*
> *Transport to Mill.*
> *Milling.*
> *Other Departments requiring Power.*

The quantity of important Stores used, though not the cash amount :—

> Spare Parts.
> Lubricant, &c.

These pass through the Stores Account, in common with all other Stores. The Foreman should always be cognizant of what is being consumed and what is on hand.

Stock of Vaporizing Oil.

The Oil for fuel passes through the Stores Accounts, in common with all other Stores. The Engineer in charge, however, should always be cognizant of what is consumed and what is on hand.

The Oil Account should always be checked in its total debits by the Accountant by reference to this sheet.

Stock of Vaporizing Oil should be noted in the Remarks column monthly, as follows :—

Stock of Oil brought forward from last month,	...	gallons.
Quantity added to Stock during month,	... ...	,,
Total available, ...		,,
Consumed during this month, ...		,,
Stock carried forward to next month,	... ...	,,

Renewals or Repairs.

Notes to be made in the Remarks column of any repairs which have been made during the month that have not been reported in Form **G**, so that in the Expenditure Sheet (No. 8) they may be charged to **MAINTENANCE OF PLANT.**

Specimen.

See pages 83 and 84.

Copies for the Head Office.

A copy of the Power Report Book **Fo** to be forwarded monthly to the Head Office on the Form provided for the purpose.

WORK DONE *for the*

ENGINE No. *1, driving 10 Stamp Mill and Breaker. Size, 25 B.H.P.*

DATE.	Time Run. Hours.	Revolutions. Daily Number.	Consumpt of Vaporizing Oil. Gallons.	Load.
May 1	24	244,080	50	10 Stamps working.
,, 2	24	244,060	49	10 ,, ,,
,, 3	24	244,000	49	10 ,, ,,
,, 4	22	223,600	45	10 ,, ,,
,, 5	24	244,020	49	10 ,, ,,
,, 6	12	122,000	24	10 ,, ,,

3

Month of May, 1896.

Quality and Brand of Oil used, K. W. O. Oil—Flash Point, 140°.

REMARKS.

Stopped two hours to repair belt.

Date,.....................................

....

Mechanical Engineer.

Maintenance of Plant.

Form **G.**

Responsible Officer.—The Mechanical or Construction Engineer.

The design of this book is to shew the work done by the Mechanical Engineer in repairing or up-keeping the plant, when repairs are carried out by a repairing or maintenance staff of mechanics outside of the individual mechanics or enginemen in charge of the working of the plant.

When repairs are done by the latter they are reported on the other Departmental Working Forms.

Entries for this Book.

To be made from time to time, as the work progresses, from the Time Books and notes kept by the workmen employed on the jobs.

Entries in this book should shew the following :—

The total number of men and the jobs on which they were employed during the month by this department.

This should be compared with the number of men charged in the Wages Sheet to this department.

The total sum charged to Wages Account under this department, in men's names, should be equal to the total sum distributed out in the above.

The quantity of important Stores used, though not the cash amount.

The distribution of work done charged in the Expenditure Sheet (No. **8**), page 149, should be made as follows, under the head of

MAINTENANCE OF PLANT.

MINING—
> *Pumping Gear.*
> *Rock Drills and Compressors.*

HAULAGE—
> *Hauling Gear.*
> *Underground Tramway.*
> *Main Shaft.*
> *Houses over Hauling Engines.*

TRANSPORT—
> *Maintenance of Tramways.*

MILLING—
> *Mills, Rock-breakers, &c.*
> *Houses over Mills.*

CYANIDING—
> *Sands Plant.*
> *Slimes Plant.*
> *Houses over Cyanide Plant.*

OFFICES—
> *Counting-house, Laboratory, and Drawing Office.*
> *Store Buildings and Stables.*
> *Staff Quarters.*

FOR GOLD MINING BUSINESS.

POWER—

  Pumping Engines and Boilers.

  Hauling Engines and Boilers.

  Hydraulic Power, including Mill-race.

  Mill Engines and Boilers.

  Dynamos, Motors, and Transformers.
  Electric Cable Lines.
  Switchboards and Instruments.

  Oil Engines.

Specimen.

  See pages 87 and 88.

Copies for the Head Office.

  A copy of the Maintenance of Plant Book **G** to be forwarded monthly to the Head Office in the Form provided for the purpose.

WORK DONE *for the Month of*

Date Beginning.	Date Ending.	DEPARTMENT.	WORK DONE.
		Milling.	Twenty Stamp Mill. Hung up 5 head; 5 hours replacing broken cam.
		Milling.	Twenty Stamp Mill Engine. Stopped 6 hours—stripping main bearing brasses and packing glands.
		Cyaniding.	Re-erecting Vat No. 11.

FOR GOLD MINING BUSINESS.

MECHANICS EMPLOYED.	Material Used.	REMARKS.
1 Mechanic, 5 hours; and	One new cam.	
4 Kaffirs' time, 15 hours,		
2 Mechanics, 6 hours,	3 lbs. packing.	
2 Carpenters, 208 hours,		
10 Kaffirs, 1000 hours,		

> ### 𝔑ote.
> **Erection of New Plant.**
> This Form may be used when New Plant is being erected; but different sheets should be taken, so as to keep separate records.

Date.......................................

.... Mechanical Engineer.

RULES AND SPECIMENS

OF

THE ACCOUNT BOOKS.

Introduction.

THE Staff Arrangements and the Departmental or Technical Reports of Work done having been treated of in the previous pages, the Accounts and the method of recording and summarizing Departmental Expenditure now remain to be dealt with.

As in the case of the Working Reports, the Specimen Account Books are preceded by notes on the writing up of the books and kindred matters to which they respectively refer. These should be inserted at the beginning of each book in use, so that they may be constantly before the Responsible Officer who has charge of it. In the case of an Assistant Clerk keeping any of these books, his name should be written in the place indicated for this purpose.

The compiler would here remark that the illustrations given are not intended to teach book-keeping, nor in any sense to supersede the intelligent work of Accountants, either professional or otherwise, but are simply practical suggestions for securing some uniform system. The distinctive feature of the system of accounts here recommended is, that the classification of the whole expenditure be restricted to the four accounts—Wages, Stores Issued, General Charges, and Sundries—leaving the departmental figures to be dealt with in the form of a schedule (see pages 161 and 166).

The Specimen Ledger has been posted up for the month of January only, but in the principal accounts figures for a whole year are given as specimens.

It is recommended that the head of each department should be supplied every month with a statement of the expenditure in his department rated out to shew the cost per ton, foot, or as the case may be. The practice has been found, in the experience of the compiler, productive of good results.

The diagram given on page 40 shews the distribution of the Cash and Stores to the different departments.

Cash Book.

Form I.

Requisitions for Money.

As the money required for wages, &c., is provided by remittances from the Head Office, ample notice should be given by the Commercial Superintendent of amounts required.

Bank Account is to be kept with the...

in the name of the Company; and all cheques are to be signed by the General Manager, and countersigned by the Commercial Superintendent or the Accountant

Bank Certificate of Balance at end of each month is to be sent to Head Office as a Voucher; and a memorandum (when necessary) reconciling the balance as shewn in the Cash Book with the amount in the Bank Certificate.

Responsible Officer.—The Accountant or Cashier.

To be written up by

Entries.

All payments of Accounts or receipts of money are to be duly entered individually in the Cash Book under their proper dates, with the name of the persons to whom paid or of whom received. In the Head Office copy of the Cash Book, the General Charges should be brought in at the end, grouped together in the manner shewn, but with the necessary particulars set out in detail.

All Accounts, and even wages, should, if possible, be paid by cheques.

Duplicate Vouchers are to be obtained in all cases, one of which is to be sent on to Head Office.

Under no circumstances should the Cash Book be kept open beyond the proper closing date in order to include payments which have not truly been made on or before the last day of each month.

Postings.

To the MINES LEDGER (No. 5):—

The various Debits and Credits throughout the month, together with the totals of the Cash and Bank columns (see pages 131 and 132).

It is intended that all outlays chargeable against Stores should be dealt with through the Purchase Day Book.

Specimen.

See pages 93 and 94.

Copies for the Head Office.

A copy of the Cash Book to be forwarded monthly to the Head Office on the Form provided for the purpose.

SPACE RESERVED FOR MS. NOTES.

Dr.   *For the Month of*

			Ledger Folio.		Cash.			Bank.		
					£	s.	d.	£	s.	d.
895. Jan.	1	To BALANCE *on hand and in Bank,*			76	9	6	643	4	6
„	10	„ JAMES THOMSON,	144		„	19	4			
„	„	„ ROBERT ANDERSON,	144		7	„	„			
„	31	„ LONDON OFFICE ACCOUNT—								
		Draft, dated	132					1000	„	„
„	„	„ BANK ACCOUNT—*withdrawn from Bank,*			750	„	„			
					£834	8	10	£1643	4	6

TOTAL DEBITS *for Month—*

Cash Account,	£757 19 4	131
Bank Account,	1000 „ „	131

January, 1895.   **Cr.**

		Voucher No.	Ledger Folio.	Cash.			Bank.		
				£	s.	d.	£	s.	d.
5	*By* JAMES WHITE,	53	143	1	4	11			
6	„ SUNDRY WORKMEN FOR WAGES—								
	Balance for December,		139	232	1	6			
17	„ JOHN BLACK & CO.,	54	143				104	„	„
20	„ THOMAS BROWN,	55	143				15	„	„
31	„ PERKINS & WEBB,	56	143	100	0	„			
„	„ CASH ACCOUNT—*per Contra,*						750	„	„
„	„ SUNDRY WORKMEN FOR WAGES—								
	A/c January,		139	433	2	1			
„	„ GENERAL CHARGES ACCOUNT—								

	Cash.	Bank.			
Salaries—					
Wm. Robertson,		£50 „ „	57		
D. Jamieson,		33 6 8	58		
		£83 6 8			
Other Charges— (Giving necessary details under each heading.)					
Travelling Expenses,	£ 2 „ „		59		
Postages,	1 1 10				
Cablegrams,		5 „ „	60		
Exchange on Draft,		10 „ „			
		£98 6 8			
		3 1 10			
Total,	£101 8 6		135	3 1 10	98 6 8

		Voucher No.	Ledger Folio.	Cash.			Bank.		
„	„ Balance on hand and in Bank,			64	12	6	675	17	10
				£834	8	10	£1643	4	6

TOTAL CREDITS *for Month*—

Cash Account,	£769 16 4	132
Bank Account,	967 6 8	132

Wages.
Note.
These will appear Weekly, Fortnightly, or Monthly, according to method of payment.

Date,................ ....

.... *Accountant.*

94

Credit or Purchase Day Book.

Form **2.**

Responsible Officer.—The Accountant.

To be written up by

....

Entries.

Purchases of every kind during the month, together with cost of Transport, Insurance, &c., are to be entered in full detail in this book, after having been carefully checked and certified as under :—

1. That the goods are in conformity with the order given (see page 19) as to quantity and price charged. This is the duty of the Accountant.

2. That the quantity received is the same as the quantity invoiced. This should be counted independently by the Stores Clerk before he is shewn the invoice, and a note of the quantities handed to the Accountant.

3. Quality should be checked by the General Manager or by some one appointed by him.

4. Calculations should all be checked by the Accountant or some one appointed by him.

5. The final passing should be done by the Manager, who has thus the first and last check on all purchases.

The following stamp should be affixed to each Invoice, and the initials filled in as checked :—

	Initials.
Quantity and Price as Ordered, - - -	
Quantity Received as Invoiced, - - -	
Quality, - - - - -	
Calculations, - - -	
Passed by - - -	

Postings.

To the MINES LEDGER (No. **5**) :—

The CREDITS throughout the month to be posted to the credit of the Personal Accounts.

The totals of these items, properly grouped together, give the DEBIT Postings to the General Stores and other Impersonal Accounts to which they belong.

To the STORES LEDGER (No. **7**) :—

The individual DEBITS for Stores, together with all charges thereon, are also to be posted to the debit of their respective accounts in the Stores Ledger.

FOR GOLD MINING BUSINESS.

Specimen.

See pages 97 and 98.

Copies for the Head Office.

A copy of the Purchase Day Book to be forwarded monthly to the Head Office on the Form provided for the purpose.

General Ledger Folio	1895.			Stores Ledger Folio.	£	s.	d.	£	
144	Jan.	3	JAMES WHITE—						
			Three Bars Drill Steel, 3/4", 0 Cwts. 2 Qrs. 14 Lbs., at 35/,	153	1	1	11		
			Railway Carriage and Forwarding,		„	3	„		
			General Stores Account,					1	4
144		15	JOHN BLACK & CO.—						
			One 10" Centres Self-acting Lathe, (give full details,)		104	„	„		
			General Stores Account,					104	
144		17	THOMAS BROWN						
			Mining Ore, as per Contract, at Alpha Mine, 30 tons at 10/,		15	„	„		
			Sundries Account,					15	„
132		23	LONDON OFFICE—						
			For Goods shipped from U.K., per s.s. "Glenbery,"						
			as per J. Thomson & Co.'s Invoice,						
			One 12" × 24" Coupled Geared Winding Engine,						
			(full details to be entered as given in Supplier's Invoice,)		620	„	„		
			One 22 H.-P. Nominal Steel Cornish Boiler,						
			(full details to be entered as given in Supplier's Invoice,)		233	„	„		
					853	„	„		
			CHARGES.						
			Freight, £74 2 3						
			Shipping Charges, 8 15 „						
			Inspection, 12 10 „						
			Insurance on £1150 at 10/ per cent., 5 15 „		101	2	3		
			General Stores Account, Engine, £670 „ „	153					
			Boiler, 284 2 3					954	2
			Forward,					£1074	7

January, 1895.

					£	s.	d.	£	s.	d.
1895. Jan.	5			*Forward,*				1074	7	2
		PERKINS & WEBB—								
		Transport on Engine and Boiler from Coast to Mine,			100	6	„			
		General Stores Account, *Engine,* £25 6 „		153						
		Boiler, 75 „ „						100	6	„
		January.						£1174	13	2
		General Stores Account.	(*Debit,*)		1159	13	2			
		Sundries Account.	(*do.,*)		15	„	„			
					£1174	13	2			

𝔑ote.

Mining Contracts.

It will be observed in the specimen that certain work done under a *Mining Contract* has been entered in this Book. It might be better to enter such in the *Wages Book;* but the one method or the other should be adhered to.

Date,...

Accountant.

Debit or Sales Day Book.

Form 3.

This book is intended only for such occasional Sales as arise in the ordinary course of matters. Where a Store is kept by the Company for the sale of provisions to the public, the Accounts should be kept distinct from the Working Accounts of the Mining and Extraction operations.

It may be here remarked that Gold Companies rarely enter the field of Store-keepers for trading purposes, nor is it recommended. Sometimes, however, when men are working on contract, the Company supply the Stores and charge the men with such, entries for which would, of course, be passed through the Sales Day Book, and provision made by an extra column in the Wages Sheet for deducting the amount from the men's wages.

The principal entry each month, however, is that for the Stores issued to the departments. This might have been put in the Journal alongside the entry for Wages, but there are some advantages in putting it here.

Both the Purchase and Sales Day Books, therefore, stand in close relation to the General Stores Account, thus :—

> *In the* Credit or Purchase Day Book *are entered all goods coming into the concern.*
>
> *In the* Debit or Sales Day Book *are entered all goods going out of Store into use in the operations, and any occasional sales made to employés or neighbours.*

The Credit and Debit Day Books (Nos. 2 and 3) thus hold the same place in regard to Stores that the Cash Book (No. 1) holds to Cash.

Whatever other books are used, the record of the incoming and outgoing of Stores is to be rigidly kept; and with regard to the former, it is immaterial whether they are for Stock or immediate use, they should never, under any circumstances, be debited direct to a department, but always, in the first place, to the General Stores Account, and the necessary credits given to the latter for all Stores issued.

Responsible Officer.—The Accountant.

To be written up by

- -

Entries.

The Invoices of all sales during the month, are to be entered in this book. Also, for convenience, if the number of entries is small, and to avoid the use of another book, any Rents, Licenses, &c., due by sundry persons are to be entered in this book in full detail.

This book may also be conveniently used for entering the bullion sold to local banks or sent to London.

All sales of goods are to be authorized by the Manager.

Postings.

The reverse here applies to the instructions given in the Purchase Day Book, the individual items throughout the month being posted to the debit of the persons to whom the Stores were sold, or by whom rents or other charges were incurred, and the Stores issued for use in the departments debited to Stores Issued Account. The totals for the month are also, as in the Purchase Day Book, to be summarized and credited to the accounts to which they belong, the postings being therefore as follow :—

To the MINES LEDGER (No. **5**) :—
The DEBITS throughout the month to be posted to the DEBIT of the Personal Accounts.
The totals of these items, properly grouped together, give the CREDIT Postings to General Stores and other Impersonal Accounts to which they belong.

To the STORES LEDGER (No. **7**) :—
The individual CREDITS of Stores issued are also to be posted to the CREDIT of their respective accounts in the Stores Ledger. These will be found in the relative summaries of Stores Issued (No. **7a**), page 155.

Specimen.

See pages 101 and 102.

Copies for the Head Office.

A copy of the Sales Day Book to be forwarded monthly to the Head Office on the form provided for the purpose.

Ledger Folio.	1895.			Stores Ledger Folio.	£	s.	d.	£	s.	d.
143	Jan.	4	JAMES THOMSON							
			For 1 bag Lime,	153	,,	11	6			
			2 lbs. Wire Nails,		,,	,,	7			
			1 Flat Chisel,		,,	1	5			
			10 Clay Crucibles,	154	,,	5	10			
			General Stores Account,					,,	19	4
143	,,	31	ROBERT ANDERSON—							
			For 1 month's Rent of Store, &c.,							
			to		12	3	,,			
			Incidental Receipts Account,					12	3	
135	,,	31	STORES ISSUED ACCOUNT—							
			For Stores issued during month, as							
			per Summary of Stores Issued							
			Sheet, page 160.		343	4	6			
			Working Account, £343 4 6							
			Erection of New							
			Plant Account, ,, ,, ,,							
			General Stores Account,					343	4	
								£356	6	10
			Summary.							
142			General Stores Account, (*Credit*),		344	3	10			
140			Incidental Receipts Account, (do.),		12	3	,,			
					£356	6	10			

January, 1895.

Note.

Profits on Sales of Stores.

In the illustration given no profit has been taken, but any profits made in this way form a credit to Incidental Receipts Account, the net amount only being credited to Stores Account.

Bullion Shipments or Sales.

This book should also be used to record any Sales of Gold to Local Banks or Shipments of Gold to London. In the latter case the ounces only are filled in by way of a memorandum, which may be put after the summary.

Date,..

Accountant.

Journal.

Form **4.**

Responsible Officer.—The Accountant.

To be written up by

_____

Entries.

It is desirable, for many reasons, to restrict, as far as possible, the entries in this book. The wages entry is, of course, the most important of the regular monthly entries; but other entries may arise from time to time. With the exception of these, however, and the closing entries for the year, specimens of which are also given, there is little else which should require journalizing, as the posting of both the DEBITS and CREDITS of the Purchase and Sales Books are made direct from these books, and the departmental figures are all dealt with in the Expenditure or allocation Schedules.

Specimen.

See pages 105 and 106.

Copies for the Head Office.

A copy of the Journal to be forwarded monthly to the Head Office on the Form provided for the purpose.

SPACE RESERVED FOR MS. NOTES.

Specimen of the Entries for the month of January, 1895.

1895.				Ledger Folio.	£	s.	d.	£	s.
Jan.	31	GENERAL CHARGES ACCOUNT,	DR.	135	65	"	"		
		TO LONDON OFFICE ACCOUNT,		142				65	
		For amount advanced to E. Thomson on Account of							
		Travelling Expenses to Mine,							
	31	WAGES ACCOUNT,	DR.	133	564	4	7		
		TO SUNDRY WORKMEN,		140				564	4
		For Wages for month of January, as per Wages Sheet (No. 6)—							
		Working Account, £564 4 7							
		Erection of New Plant A/c., " " "							

NOTE (1).—*When the work is largely in the hands of a Contractor, the payments to him should be shown in a separate Ledger Account, in which case the Wages Entry would be as follows:—*

		WAGES ACCOUNT,	DR.		564	4	7		
		TO SUNDRY WORKMEN,						363	10
		J. WATSON, Contractor,						201	9

NOTE (2).—*It sometimes happens that Wages appear in the sheets chargeable against Stores for handling charges, and, in some cases, for skilled employés making up certain articles for use. A simple way of dealing with such is to debit the amount direct to Stores A/c., as follows:—*

		WAGES ACCOUNT,	DR.		502	"	1		
		GENERAL STORES ACCOUNT,	DR.		62	4	6		
		(With the necessary subsidiary postings to the Stores Ledger.)							
		TO SUNDRY WORKMEN,						564	4

Specimen of the Closing Entries for the Year 1895.

		Ledger Folio.	£	s.	d.	£	s.	d.
35. 31	GENERAL WORKING ACCOUNT, DR.	137	19,098	13	1			
	TO SUNDRIES—							
	For Expenditure during year ending							
	WAGES ACCOUNT, *see Expenditure Summary, page 170,*	134				8,042	4	10
	STORES ISSUED ACCOUNT, „ „	136				8,685	12	2
	GENERAL CHARGES ACCOUNT, „ „	130				2,172	„	5
	SUNDRIES ACCOUNT, „ „	138				198	17	8
31	MOVABLE PLANT ACCOUNT, DR.	143	193	19	„			
	TO GENERAL WORKING ACCOUNT,	138				193	19	„
	For amount of Inventory at 31st Dec., 1895, in excess							
	of Inventory at 31st Dec., 1894.							
31	ERECTION OF NEW PLANT ACCOUNT, DR.	149	3,952	5	11			
	TO SUNDRIES—							
	For Expenditure during year ending							
	WAGES ACCOUNT, *see Expenditure Summary, page 170,*	134				1,908	7	8
	STORES ISSUED ACCOUNT, „ „	136				2,043	18	3
31	WORKS, BUILDINGS, AND FIXED PLANT ACCOUNT, DR.	123	3,952	5	11			
	TO SUNDRIES—							
	For Amount transferred,	149				3,952	5	11
	The whole amount being, in this case, transferred to the							
	former Account in terms of the Engineer's Report							
	(see page 129).							
	See also instruction as to shewing additions in Annual							
	Inventories (page 114).							

Date,...............

....*Accountant.*

Specimen of the Closing Entries for the Year 1895—continued.

				Ledger Folio.	£	s.	d.	£	s.
Dec.	31	SUNDRIES—	DR.						
		TO LONDON OFFICE ACCOUNT—							
		For Amounts transferred,		132				42	7
		UNCLAIMED WAGES ACCOUNT,		141	17	12	9		
		INCIDENTAL RECEIPTS ACCOUNT,		139	24	15	,,		
,,	31	LONDON OFFICE ACCOUNT,	DR.	131	18,904	14	1		
		TO GENERAL WORKING ACCOUNT,		138				18,904	14
		For Balance at 31st Dec., 1895, transferred.							
,,	31	LONDON OFFICE ACCOUNT,	DR.	131	1,182	,,	,,		
		TO WORKS, BUILDINGS, AND FIXED PLANT ACCOUNT,		134				1,182	,,
		For Depreciation, at rate of 7½ per cent., on							
		£15,754 16s. 8d.—being Balance at Debit of							
		this Account at 31st December, 1894.							

FOR GOLD MINING BUSINESS.

Date.......

Accountant.

The Mines Ledger.

Form **5.**

Responsible Officer.—The Accountant.

To be written up by

....

Entries.

Only postings from the four books previously referred to, namely :—

> No. 1.—CASH BOOK,
> „ 2.—PURCHASE DAY BOOK,
> „ 3.—SALES DAY BOOK,
> „ 4.—JOURNAL,

should find their way into the Mines Ledger. All transfer entries other than the regular closing entries should be avoided as far as possible.

List of Accounts to be opened and the order to be observed.

> **London or Head Office Account.**
> **Bank Account.**
> **Cash Account.**
> **General Stores Account.**

> **Works, Buildings, and Fixed Plant Account.**
> **Movable Plant Account.**
> **Live Stock Account.**

> **Wages Account.**
> **Stores Issued or Used Account.**
> **General Charges Account.**
> **Sundries Account.**

> **General Working Account.**
> **Erection of New Plant Account.**
> **Sundry Workmen Account.**
> **Unclaimed Wages Account.**
> **Incidental Receipts Account.**
> **Personal Accounts, as required in separate section**
> **of the book.**

Notes

On the respective Accounts will be found on pages 111 to 130.

Ledger Balances.

A list of Ledger Balances to be furnished to Head Office monthly, or as periodically arranged.

FOR GOLD MINING BUSINESS.

SPACE RESERVED FOR MS. NOTES.

London or Head Office Account.

Entries.

The CREDITS would consist chiefly of remittances and store shipments. The principal DEBITS would arise at the close of the year.

Specimen.

See page 131.

𝔑𝔬𝔱𝔢.

The "**Mines Account**" kept in the Head Office Ledger should be exactly the reverse of the "**Head Office Account**" kept in the Mines Ledger; but there are often, of course, items of Cash and Stores in transit to be reckoned in adjusting the two accounts.

As all the Working Accounts in the Mines Books (Wages, Stores Issued, &c.) are closed off at the end of the year to the London Office Account, the net balance remaining at credit of latter, say on 1st January of any year, should represent simply the various assets at the Mine on that date (excluding, of course, the Mines Property itself, which is a Head Office Account), less the liabilities, if any.

Bank Account.

Entries.

The monthly totals of cash paid into Bank and cash withdrawn from Bank, to be posted to Dr. and Cr. of this Account, and the balance agreed with the Bank column of the Cash Book from which the postings are taken in the manner shewn.

Specimen.

See page 131.

General Stores Account.

Entries.

These come almost entirely from the

PURCHASE DAY BOOK and
SALES DAY BOOK ;

in which case the DEBIT ENTRIES consist of the monthly totals of Stores purchased, as per Purchase Day Book.

The CREDIT ENTRIES consist of the monthly totals of Stores issued and sold, as per Sales Day Book.

Occasional Entries, however, arise in the Cash Book and Journal.

The account itself must, of course, be kept in exact agreement with the Stores Ledger; the latter being simply a series of the respective "Store" accounts, which, in the aggregate, correspond to the above account. Care must be taken, therefore, that every posting, whether Debit or Credit to the above account, must also have a subsidiary or duplicate posting to some account in the Stores Ledger.

INVENTORIES—Goods in Store.

Inventories of all stores on hand should be made up at least once in every year. These should be verified, as far as possible, by the Manager and Commercial Superintendent, and countersigned by them. The balance at Debit of this account, and also the Stores Ledger Balances, should be brought into agreement therewith.

The "Stores Used" to be charged out at cost price or as near to it as possible, but any differences arising between the Stores Ledger Balances and the Inventories should be adjusted at stocktaking, and advised to the Head Office.

In no case should the values adopted in the Inventories be made to agree with the Stores Ledger. The latter should be corrected as required; that is to say, presuming that at stocktaking it is discovered that an error has been made during the year, either in the quantity issued or in the price charged, the stock at the end of the year is to be impartially valued as it stands, at cost or under, if necessary, and an adjusting Journal Entry made to correct the error which has occurred, the proper department being duly debited or credited with the amount.

INVENTORIES—Goods in Transit.

Any return of this kind should give date of the Head Office advice, or colonial suppliers' advice, from which the items are taken and such other particulars as will enable the "transit" or shipment from London, &c., to be readily identified.

Specimen.

See page 131.

Works, Buildings, and Fixed Plant Account.

Entries.

FROM THE JOURNAL.—As the additions to these are taken from the Erection of New Plant Account, there should be, as a rule, only two entries yearly affecting this account :—viz.,

1. Transfer of approved amount from Erection of New Plant Account.
2. Amount written off for depreciation, which, in the yearly inventories, should be shewn in a separate column.

From the SALES DAY BOOK.—It sometimes happens that a sale of a piece of machinery is made to a neighbouring Company, which would necessitate an entry being made in the Sales Day Book, debiting the purchaser and crediting this account with the value obtained. The difference between the realized value and the book value should be transferred to Head Office Account.

INVENTORY.

It is important here, with regard both to uniformity and comparison of Inventories of plant, that the particular arrangement or classification adopted in the Accounts should be strictly adhered to year by year. These Inventories should be made up in columns, shewing (*a*) Value at previous stocktaking, (*b*) Additions during year, (*c*) Depreciation, (*d*) Present value.

Specimen.

See page 133.

Movable Plant Account.

Entries.

From the SALES DAY BOOK.—When a property (or mine) is being equipped with movable plant—such as picks, shovels, hammers, &c., &c., and office and dwelling-house furnishing—the articles so issued should be debited, at the outset, to Movable Plant Account.

Should any article become worn out during the year, and require to be replaced, the new article issued from Store in its place must be charged against its proper department in the General Working Account, and not to Movable Plant Account.

By this system Movable Plant Account in the Ledger is not altered throughout the year; any variations being adjusted yearly when the Inventory is made up.

Presuming, however, that during the year work was begun on a new section or department, necessitating the issue of additional tools and sundry movable plant, these items would be debited to Movable Plant Account, as they would constitute a real addition to the stock of movable plant, in contradistinction to a renewal of something that had already been debited to movable plant, but had become worn out.

INVENTORY.

At the end of the financial year an Inventory should be taken of the movable plant (see remarks on previous page as to classification), the various items in use on the property being carefully valued according to their condition, and the whole certified by the General Manager and Commercial Superintendent. The difference between the total valuation and the amount standing at the debit of movable plant in the Ledger will represent the amount which should be written off or credited to General Working Account, and apportioned to the departments to which it is chargeable.

Specimen.

See page 133.

Live Stock Account.

INVENTORY.

An Inventory of live stock should be made up at the end of each financial year.

FOR GOLD MINING BUSINESS.

SPACE RESERVED FOR MS. NOTES.

Wages Account.

Entries.

DEBIT ENTRIES.—The total amount of Wages earned, as per pay sheet, for which credit is given to Sundry Workmen.

CREDIT ENTRIES.—These consist simply of transfers to the

General Working Account or
Erection of New Plant Account,
Movable Plant Account,
Live Stock Account,

as the case may be, and should be left till the end of the year, when the whole can be transferred in one entry.

With the view of getting always the Wages earned into the month to which they are properly chargeable, a Journal Entry is made, debiting the Wages Account and crediting Sundry Workmen, the actual payments being then debited to the latter account.

It is recommended that payments should be limited to a particular pay day.

In the case of particular contracts it may be advisable to open an account for the contractor, see specimen entry on page 91 in the Journal.

Where also any part of the wages is chargeable against General Stores Account, for handling charges, &c., it should be split up as in the Journal Entry shewn.

Specimens.

See page 133.

Stores Issued or Stores Used Account.

Entries.

DEBIT ENTRIES.—The monthly totals of Stores used in process, as ordered by the Foremen, and summarized through Form No. **7a,** are posted to the debit of this account from the Sales Day Book (see page 101).

CREDIT ENTRIES.—These consist simply of transfers at the close of the year to the

General Working Account or
Erection of New Plant Account,
Movable Plant Account,
Live Stock Account,

as the case may be, and should be left till the end of the year, when the whole can be transferred in one entry.

Specimen.

See page 135.

General Charges Account.

This account is intended for Salaries and other expenses of the kind indicated below, which should always be classified under sub-headings in the Cash Book or other book in which they occur. Only the totals need be posted to the Ledger Account, but an Abstract should accompany the Head Office Returns monthly or yearly, as required.

Sub-Headings.

> **Staff Salaries,**
> **Cablegrams,**
> **Postages and Telegrams,**
> **Government Taxes and Dues,**
> **Rent,**
> **Travelling Expenses,**
> **Legal Expenses,**
> **Medical Expenses,**
> **Gratuities,**
> **Bank Charges,**
> **&c.**

In the General Expenditure Sheet these Charges are, for convenience, given under the heading of Office, Store, &c.

Entries.

Arise chiefly in the Cash Book, but may also occur in the Purchase Day Book or Journal.

Specimen.

See page 135.

Sundries Account.

This Account, as distinguished from General Charges Account, is intended for such exceptional items of expenditure as do not properly come under any of the other three heads of Wages, Stores Issued, and General Charges, as, for instance, work done by contractors, who would be credited through the Purchase Day Book. Such expenditure would be debited in the Ledger to Sundries Account, and would appear in the "Sundries" column of the General Expenditure Sheet opposite its proper Department.

In like manner, the charge for Native Passes would be debited to Sundries Account, and credited to the Mining Commissioner through the Purchase Day Book.

Specimen.

See page 137.

General Working Account.

Entries.

The principal, and almost the only entries in this Account, are those arising at the end of the year from the transfer of the four General Expenditure Accounts—Wages, Stores Issued, General Charges, and Sundries, and the closing of the Account by transfer to the Head Office Account.

INVENTORY.

An Inventory of the Stock of Ore on hand lying either at the Dump at the Mine, or at the Bins at the Rock Breakers, and not yet delivered for treatment should be made out at the end of the year, the Ore to be valued strictly at cost of mining, with cost of delivery at the Bins included, if it has been delivered there, provided always that this cost can be realized in treatment. This amount would be credited to General Working Account, and carried forward as a debit to next year in the manner shewn on page 137.

Specimen.

See page 137.

Bullion Account.

Any local sales of Bullion would form a credit to this account, the debtors being the Local Bank or Mint. The value of Bullion on hand at close of year would form a credit to this account, and be carried forward to next year's account as a stock on hand.

Arrangements should be made to have the plates cleaned up and scraped at the close of the year, so as to bring all the Gold obtained into the year's accounts.

Specimen.

No specimen of this account is given.

FOR GOLD MINING BUSINESS.

Erection of New Plant Account.

Entries.

In the system of book-keeping here recommended the amount expended on new plant (or in any particular department) is shewn only in the Allocation Schedules (see General Expenditure Sheet, Form **8**). The entries for this account, therefore, consists simply of transfers at the end of the year from the four Expenditure Accounts, and the transfer of these again to Works, Buildings, and Fixed Plant Account, so far as authorized by the Consulting Engineer.

Specimen.

See page 139.

Unclaimed Wages Account.

Entries.

When Wages have been unclaimed for a length of time it is well to transfer the amount from Sundry Workmen Account to Unclaimed Wages Account, and advise the Head Office as to same.

Incidental Receipts Account.

Entries.

The CREDITS to this account consist chiefly of *Rents, Fines, Diggers' Licenses, Assaying done for outsiders, &c.,* and would come either from the Sales Day Book or Cash Book.

Sundry Workmen Account.

Entries.

See Wages Account and Unclaimed Wages Account.

SPACE RESERVED FOR MS. NOTES.

SPECIAL YEARLY RETURNS.

These should include, at least, the following :—

The following points should also be attended to :—

YEARLY RETURNS.

    All Accounts and Returns made up at the end of the year should deal with the same figures, and be on the same lines as the Monthly Returns, otherwise it is difficult for the Head Office to agree them. In all cases " Returns," monthly or otherwise, should be duly dated and signed by the officer responsible for them.

ORDINARY RETURNS.

    The Ordinary Returns for the last month of each financial year should never be delayed for the other Special Returns made up then, as the Head Office work is thereby unnecessarily delayed, as also the drafts of the printed accounts for the year.

OUTSTANDING LIABILITIES AT END OF FINANCIAL YEAR.

    There is less chance, perhaps, of liabilities for Stores being omitted than for *Skilled Services, Rent, Taxes, Contracts, Claims. &c.*, but care should be taken to include liabilities of every kind, as well as outstanding assets.

On the following pages will be found notes on Development, Redemption of Capital, Depreciation of Plant, and a Form of Engineer's Certificate for Erection of New Plant and Report on Value of Plant in use—all of which should come under consideration at the time of the Yearly Balance.

DEVELOPMENT.

Expenditure under this head is sometimes charged direct to current mining costs; in other cases it is carried to a separate account and held in suspense, to be afterwards gradually written off by a tonnage charge against ore raised.

In any case, only the expenditure under the first three headings on pages 163, 164 should be treated as coming under this designation.

It is sounder policy, whenever reasonably practicable, to avoid such suspense accounts, and to adopt the former plan, as is shewn in the illustrations given herein; but there are cases, such as the deep level mines on the Rand, and in other mines, where a large initial expenditure has to be made on expensive shafts, and in the blocking out of great reserves of ore a year or two ahead. In these cases it is admissible to write off the cost of development by a tonnage charge against ore mined, the rate being fixed from time to time by dividing the balance outstanding as cost of development by the number of tons actually developed.

Great care is necessary in these cases to see that the mine costs are not unduly reduced by an insufficient charge per ton for the redemption of the Development Account.

REDEMPTION OF CAPITAL.

Mining properties differ from ordinary industrial undertakings in this respect, that apart from the ordinary wear and tear of buildings, machinery, and plant which all such enterprises must provide for, a mine is itself a "wasting" property, of which the "corpus" diminishes and eventually disappears.

It is true that there are exceptional cases in which the ore bodies are, in the common phrase, "practically inexhaustible;" but, in a general way, provision must be made for the eventual replacement of the capital employed when the "life" of the mine is exhausted.

What the life of a mine should be estimated at is a matter requiring the best technical advice, and no pains should be spared in arriving at a sound conclusion. In some cases, where claims are bounded by vertical lines, and the reefs dip at considerable angles, a fairly close estimate can be made. When a reef is vertical, or the mining laws allow it to be followed on the dip outside the side lines of the claims, there is more opening for judgment and discretion in deciding the possible depth to which it may be worked.

It is beyond the scope of this work to discuss, in detail, the mode of estimating the period at the end of which the capital should be replaced. This having been determined upon technical advice, prudent management requires that corresponding provision be made out of the profits of the concern for redemption, or, as it is sometimes called, amortization, apart from an ordinary reserve fund, which may be required for other objects.

Theoretically the proper course is to set aside each year out of the profits such a sum, proportionate to the ore extracted, as will, when the estimated contents of the mine have been exhausted, provide a fund equivalent to the capital expended in the purchase and equipment of same.

DEPRECIATION OF PLANT.

A usual all-round rate of depreciation is 7½ per cent., which, if applied to the original cost, would wipe off the account in about fourteen years, exclusive of any question of interest. If applied to the annually decreasing balance, it would never, of course, be exhausted; but whatever method is adopted, care should be taken that the remaining Book Balance is not lost sight of in charging up any renewal expenditure.

Referring to the life of plant, very often it happens that changes occur in processes and machinery long before they are worn out; and in such cases as these, very much heavier writing off should be made. This, however, cannot be done by any arithmetical plan, but must be specially written off each year.

In addition to the 7½ per cent. which comes off every item, the General Manager or Consulting Engineer should recommend, for the consideration of the Board, every year, any plant which he thinks should have a special depreciation written off it, so that the Board in London may deal with it accordingly.

Sometimes a Depreciation Account is kept for every different machine, so as to be dealt with separately; and there is no doubt that this principle is a good one, and should be adopted where the staff are sufficiently skilled, and careful to follow it up properly.

In adopting an all-round rate for depreciation, the rate must be fixed at a figure that will bear comparison with separate rates of separate classes of machinery.

SPECIMEN OF CERTIFIED STATEMENT OF CAPITAL EXPENDITURE
for the year ending 31st December, 1895.

BUILDINGS.

OFFICE, STORE, &c.

Laboratory	...	(see page.. of Yearly Summary Bk.,)	£151	7	,,		
Office and Store,	,,	,,	,,	204	18	10	
Staff Quarters,	,,	,,	,,	184	13	7	
CYANIDE VATS—*Foundations, &c.*	..	,,	1,613	18	11		
						£2,154	18 4

MACHINERY AND FIXED PLANT.

TRAMWAYS,	...	...	(see page ..of Yearly Summary Bk.,)	£555	18	1	
CYANIDE PLANT,	...	,,	,,	,,	188	10	9
MILLING PLANT,	...	,,	,,	,,	132	18	5
POWER—*Hydraulic Works,* ,,		,,	,,	920	,,	4	
						1,797	7 7
						£3,952	5 11

ENGINEER'S CERTIFICATE.

I have carefully inspected the additions to Plant and Buildings during the year ending 31st December, 1895, the expenditure on which amounts, as per Erection of New Plant Account, to £3,952 5s. 11d. The whole of this amount, I find, is chargeable against Capital Expenditure, in accordance with the above statement, and I certify that it is fully represented by Buildings, Machinery, and Plant additional to what existed at 31st December, 1894.*

I certify also that, in my opinion, there has been no abnormal depreciation of the Company's property, as per Inventories herewith, during this period, nor any loss, damage, &c., to same. (*Adding, if need be, the words "excepting as follows."*)

(*Signed*) ....

Date, 31st January, 1896.   *Consulting Engineer.*

NOTE.——If there is no Consulting Engineer, the General Manager should sign this Certificate.

---

* See remarks on previous page as to Renewals.

SPACE RESERVED FOR MS. NOTES.

Dr.   **London Office**

1895.				Folio.			
Dec.	31	To GENERAL WORKING ACCOUNT, as per Journal,		107	£18,904	14	
„	31	„ WORKS, BUILDINGS, and FIXED PLANT ACCOUNT for Depreciation					
		for year 1895, as per Journal,		107	1,182		
„	31	„ BALANCE,			3,695		
					£53,781	18	

Dr.   **Bank**

1895.					Folio.			
Jan.	1	To BALANCE brought forward,				£645	4	
„	31	„ CASH—Amount paid into Bank during month,		C. B.,	95	1,600	„	

Dr.   **Cash**

1895.				Folio.			
Jan.	1	To BALANCE brought forward,			£76	9	
„	31	„ SUNDRY RECEIPTS for month, as per Cash Book,		93	757	19	

Dr.   **General Stores**

1895.							Folio.			
Jan.	1	To BALANCE, as per Inventory at 31st December, 1894,						£8,110	16	
„	31	„ PURCHASES, &c., for Month, as per Purchase Day Book,					98	1,159	13	
Feb.	28	„	„	„	„	„	×	1,250	18	
Mar.	31	„	„	„	„	„	×	1,035	14	
April	30	„	„	„	„	„	×	1,156	19	
May	31	„	„	„	„	„	×	1,195	1	
June	30	„	„	„	„	„	×	1,194	18	
July	31	„	„	„	„	„	×	1,100	1	
Aug.	31	„	„	„	„	„	×	1,075	2	
Sept.	30	„	„	„	„	„	×	1,079	10	
Oct.	31	„	„	„	„	„	×	1,124	13	
Nov.	30	„	„	„	„	„	×	1,040	8	
Dec.	31	„	„	„	„	„	×	1,031	16	

NOTE.—Debits from Journal or Cash Book would be described accordingly.

1896.								£16,375	13	
Jan.	1	„ BALANCE, as per Inventory at 31st December, 1895,						£5,600	16	

Account.   Cr.

85,			Folio.	Journal.			Folio.	Cash Book.			Folio.	Purchase Day Book.			TOTAL.		
Nov.	1	By BALANCE,													£21,720	8	11
„	31	„ SUNDRIES,	105	665	„	„	94	£1,000	„	„	97	£954	2	3	2,019	2	3
Dec.	31	„ „	107	42	7	9									42	7	9
															£23,781	18	11

Account.   Cr.

85,					Folio.			
Dec.	31	By CASH—Amount withdrawn during month,		C. B.,	94	£967	6	8

Account.   Cr.

85,				Folio.			
Dec.	31	By SUNDRY PAYMENTS for month, as per Cash Book,		94	£769	16	4

Account.   Cr.

85,			Folio	Stores Sold.			Stores Issued to Departments.			TOTAL.		
Jan.	31	By STORES ISSUED for month, as per Sales Day Book,	101	4	19	4	£345	4	6	£344	5	10
Feb.	28	„ „ „ „	x	4	5	„	536	5	11	530	10	11
Mar.	31	„ „ „ „	x	2	3	9	776	14	8	778	16	10
April	30	„ „ „ „	x	10	„	„	939	6	8	939	6	8
May	31	„ „ „ „	x	1	7	6	1,176	3	4	1,177	10	10
June	30	„ „ „ „	x	7	3	4	1,046	16	8	1,054	„	„
July	31	„ „ „ „	x	„	15	6	903	2	2	903	17	8
Aug	31	„ „ „ „	x	„	5	9	751	17	10	752	3	7
Sep.	30	„ „ „ „	x	2	2	1	806	3	5	808	5	6
Oct.	31	„ „ „ „	x	1	4	7	952	12	1	954	16	8
Nov.	30	„ „ „ „	x	„	„	„	1,289	5	1	1,289	5	1
Dec.	31	„ „ „ „	x	6	„	4	1,227	19	1	1,233	19	5
				£56	6	7	£10,720	10	5	£10,765	17	0
	31	„ BALANCE „ INVENTORY	6							5,609	16	10
										£16,375	13	10

Dr.   Works, Buildings, and

1895.				Folio.		
Jan.	1	To BALANCE, as per Inventory of Works, Buildings, and Fixed Plant at 31st			£15,754	16
		December, 1894,				
Dec.	31	„ ERECTION OF NEW PLANT ACCOUNT. Amount transferred by authority				
		of Engineer, as per his Certificate of 31st January, 1896 (a specimen of which				
		is given on page 129),	Jo.,	106	3,952	5
1896.					£19,707	2
Jan.	1	„ BALANCE, as per Inventory at 31st December, 1895,			£18,525	2

Dr.   Movable Plant

1895.				Folio.		
Jan.	1	To BALANCE, as per Inventory of Movable Plant at 31st December, 1894,			£2,367	4
Dec.	31	„ GENERAL WORKING ACCOUNT. Amount of Inventory at 31st December,				
		1895, in excess of Inventory at 31st December, 1894,	Jo.,	106	194	19
1896.					£2,561	4
Jan.	1	„ BALANCE, as per Inventory at 31st December, 1895,			£2,561	2

Dr.   Wages

1895.				Folio.	General Working Account.			Folio.	Erection of New Plant Account.			TOTAL	
Jan.	31	To SUNDRY WORKMEN ACCOUNT, as		105	£563	4	7					£563	4
		per Journal,											
Feb.	28	„	„	„	„	x	620	10	10	x	£101	4	„	721	14
Mar.	31	„	„	„	„	x	639	13	2					639	13
April	30	„	„	„	„	x	697	2	5	x	140	2	4	837	4
May	31	„	„	„	„	x	707	9	8	x	348	4	6	1,055	12
June	30	„	„	„	„	x	687	5	4	x	431	8	9	1,018	14
July	31	„	„	„	„	x	672	1	4	x	202	12	4	874	13
Aug.	31	„	„	„	„	x	686	10	4	x	224	7	8	910	17
Sept.	30	„	„	„	„	x	664	10	9	x	160	4	„	824	14
Oct.	31	„	„	„	„	x	701	15	11	x	201	5	1	903	1
Nov.	30	„	„	„	„	x	699	10	7	x	74	„	„	773	10
Dec.	31	„	„	„	„	x	704	10	5	x	123	„	„	827	10
					£8,042	4	10		£1,908	7	8	£9,950	12

Fixed Plant Account.   Cr.

				Folio.			
	31	By LONDON OFFICE ACCOUNT. For Depreciation, at rate of 7½ per cent., on £15,752 16s. 8d., being Balance at Debit of this Account at 31st December, 1894, as per Journal,	Jo.,	107	£1,182	"	"
		„ BALANCE, as per INVENTORY at 31st December, 1895,			18,525	2	7
					£19,707	2	7

Account.   Cr.

			Folio.			
	31	By BALANCE, as per INVENTORY at 31st December, 1895,		£2,561	2	"
				£2,561	2	"

Account.   Cr.

				Folio.			
	31	By GENERAL WORKING ACCOUNT,	Jo.,	106	£8,042	4	10
	31	„ ERECTION OF NEW PLANT ACCOUNT,	Jo.,	106	1,908	7	8
					£9,950	12	6

> ### Note.
> For the Departmental allocation of the Monthly Debits, see the corresponding Wages Summary (Form 8), page 149.

Dr.   **Stores Issued**

1895.						Fol.	General Working Account.			Erection of New Plant Account.			TOTAL.		
Jan.	31	To GENERAL STORES ACCOUNT, *as per Sales*													
		Day Book,				101	£343	4	6				£343	4	6
Feb.	28	„	„	„	„	×	406	4	8	£120	1	3	526	5	
Mar.	31	„	„	„	„	×	671	6	2	105	7	6	776	14	
April	30	„	„	„	„	×	486	16	7	502	10	1	989	6	
May	31	„	„	„	„	×	662	16	„	513	7	4	1,176	3	
June	30	„	„	„	„	×	627	4	„	419	12	8	1,046	16	
July	31	„	„	„	„	×	768	2	2	135	„	„	904	2	
Aug.	31	„	„	„	„	×	651	8	7	100	9	3	751	17	
Sept.	30	„	„	„	„	×	834	15	10	61	7	7	896	3	
Oct.	31	„	„	„	„	×	952	12	1				952	12	
Nov.	30	„	„	„	„	×	1,163	2	6	98	2	7	1,189	5	
Dec.	31	„	„	„	„	×	1,227	19	1				1,227	19	
							£8,685	12	2	£2,043	18	3	£10,729	10	

Dr.   **General Charges**

1895.				Fol.	TOTAL.	
Jan.	31	To LONDON OFFICE,		105	£65	„
„	31	„ CASH,		94	101	8
Feb.	28	„ PURCHASE DAY BOOK,		×	15	10
„	28	„ CASH,		×	145	2
Mar.	31	„			166	17
April	30	„			184	13
May	31	„			196	15
June	30	„			200	14
July	31	„			210	9
Aug.	31	„			180	2
Sept.	30	„			225	„
Oct.	31	„			250	3
Nov.	30	„			175	14
Dec.	31	„			64	19
					£2,172	„

Account.

Cr.

					Folio.				
18.									
Dec.	*31*	By GENERAL WORKING ACCOUNT,		Jo.,	100	£8,685	12	2
	31	„ ERECTION OF NEW PLANT ACCOUNT,		Jo.,	100	2,048	18	3

> ### Note.
>
> For the Departmental allocation of the Monthly Debits, see the corresponding Stores Summary (Form **8**), page 160.

						£10,734	10	5

Account.

Cr.

					Folio.				
18.									
Dec.	*31*	By GENERAL WORKING ACCOUNT,		Jo.,	100	£2,172	13	5

> ### Note.
>
> The classification, &c., of the Monthly Debits should be given in an Abstract of General Charges, see note on General Expenditure Sheet (Form **8**), page 164.
>
> ----------
>
> Salaries and other Cash Charges should be all regularly paid each month, as there is no provision otherwise for getting them into the General Expenditure Sheets for the period to which they belong.

						£2,172	13	5

Dr.   **Sundries**

1895				Folio.	Erection of New Plant Account.			Folio.	General Working Account.			TOTAL		
Jan.	31	To SUNDRIES, *as per Purchase Day Book,*						98	£15	"	"	£15		
Feb.	28	,,	,,	,,	,,			x	14	7	8	14	7	
Mar.	31	,,	,,	,,	,,			x	20	16	"	20	16	
April	30	,,	,,	,,	,,			x	16	12	10	16	12	
May	31	,,	,,	,,	,,			x	12	7	5	12	7	
June	30	,,	,,	,,	,,			x	13	11	7	13	11	
July	31	,,	,,	,,	,,			x	10	4	3	10	4	
Aug.	31	,,	,,	,,	,,			x	15	10	8	15	10	
Sept.	30	,,	,,	,,	,,			x	19	2	4	19	2	
Oct.	31	,,	,,	,,	,,			x	13	15	2	13	15	
Nov.	30	,,	,,	,,	,,			x	21	2	5	21	0	
Dec.	31	,,	,,	,,	,,			x	26	5	4	26	5	
									£198	15	8	£198	17	

Dr.   **General Working**

1895.					Folio.			
Jan.	1	To *Stock of Ore not delivered for treatment, as per Inventory, brought down,*				"	"	
Dec.	31	,, SUNDRIES. *Amounts transferred from—*						
			WAGES ACCOUNT,			£8,042	4	10
			STORES ISSUED ACCOUNT,			8,685	12	2
			GENERAL CHARGES ACCOUNT,			2,172	"	5
			SUNDRIES ACCOUNT,	*Jan.,*	106	198	15	8
						£19,098	13	
						£19,098	14	

Account.   **Cr.**

95.			Folio.			
Dec. 31	By GENERAL WORKING ACCOUNT.	Jo.,	106	£198	15	8

> **Note.**
>
> For the Departmental allocation of the Monthly Debits, see the General Expenditure Sheet (Form **8**), and relative note thereon, page 164.

				£198	15	8

Account.   **Cr.**

95.			Folio.			
Dec. 31	By MOVABLE PLANT ACCOUNT. Amount in excess of Inventory at 31st December, 1895, over Inventory at 31st December, 1894,	Jo.,	106	£193	19	,,
,, 31	,, Stock of Ore not delivered for treatment, as per Inventory, carried down,			,,	,,	,,
,, 31	,, LONDON OFFICE ACCOUNT. Balance transferred,	Jo.,	107	18,904	14	1
				£19,098	13	1

Dr.   **Erection of New**

1895.				Folio.						
Dec.	31	To SUNDRIES. *Amounts transferred from—*								
		WAGES ACCOUNT,			£1,908	7	8			
		STORES ISSUED ACCOUNT,			2,043	18	3			
		GENERAL CHARGES ACCOUNT (*if any*),								
		SUNDRIES ACCOUNT (*if any*),	Jo.,	106				£3,952	5	
								£3,952	5	

Dr.   **Incidental Receipts**

1895.				Folio.			
Dec.	31	To LONDON OFFICE ACCOUNT. *Transferred,*	Jo.,	107	£24	15	
					£24	15	

Dr.   **Sundry Workmen**

1895.						Folio.			
Jan.	6	To CASH.	BALANCE *for December, 1894,*			94	£332	1	
,,	31	,, ,,	Account	,, January,		94	433	2	
Feb.	6	,, ,,	BALANCE	,, ,,		×	130	2	
,,	28	,, ,,	Account	,, February,		×	721	14	
Mar.	31	,, ,,	,,	,, March,		×	639	13	
April	30	,, ,,	,,	,, April,		×	857	4	
May	31	,, ,,	,,	,, May,		×	1,050	,,	
June	30	,, ,,	,,	,, June,		×	1,018	14	
July	31	,, ,,	,,	,, July,		×	874	13	
,,	31	,, UNCLAIMED WAGES Account	,,	,,		×	3	12	
Aug.	31	,, CASH.	Account	,, August,		×	910	17	
Sept.	30	,, ,,	,,	,, September,		×	810	14	
Oct.	31	,, ,,	,,	,, October,		×	905	1	
Nov.	30	,, ,,	,,	,, November,		×	773	10	
Dec.	31	,, ,,	,,	,, December,		×	420	8	
,,	31	,, UNCLAIMED WAGES Account	,,	,,		×	14	,,	
,,	31	,, BALANCE *carried forward*					467	2	
							£10,182	14	

Plant Account.   Cr.

1896.				Folio.			
Dec.	31	By WORKS, BUILDINGS, and FIXED PLANT ACCOUNT. Amount transferred to that Account in terms of Engineer's Certificate of 31st Jan., 1896,		106	£8,952	5	11
					£8,952	5	11

Account.   Cr.

1895.				Folio.			
Jan.	31	By SALES DAY BOOK,		101	£12	3	,,
Mar.	31	,, CASH,		×	5	10	,,
Dec.	23	,, ,,		×	7	2	,,
					£24	15	,,

Account.   Cr.

1895.				Folio.			
Jan.	1	By BALANCE brought forward,			£232	1	6
,,	31	,, WAGES ACCOUNT,		105	563	4	7
Feb.	28	,, ,,		×	721	14	10
Mar.	31	,, ,,		×	639	13	2
April	30	,, ,,		×	837	4	9
May	31	,, ,,		×	1,953	12	9
June	30	,, ,,		×	1,918	14	1
July	31	,, ,,		×	874	13	8
Aug.	31	,, ,,		×	910	17	11
Sept.	30	,, ,,		×	824	14	9
Oct.	31	,, ,,		×	966	1	,,
Nov.	30	,, ,,		×	773	10	7
Dec.	31	,, ,,		×	827	16	5
					£10,182	14	,,
Jan.	1	,, BALANCE brought forward,			£407	2	,,

> ### Note.
> Any amounts for Wages which it is not expected will be claimed, should be transferred to credit of Unclaimed Wages Account.

Dr.					Unclaimed		
895.				Folio.			
Dec.	31	To LONDON OFFICE ACCOUNT *Transferred,*	Ja.,	107	£17	12	9
					£17	12	9

Wages Account.

95.			Folio.				
July 31	By SUNDRY WORKMEN ACCOUNT,	Jo.,	×	£3	12	9
ng. 31	,, ,, ,, ,,	Jo.,	×	14	,,	,,
				£17	12	9

				Folio.			
						James	
1895. Jan.	5	To CASH,		94	£1	4	11
						John Black	
1895. Jan.	17	To CASH,		94	£104	,,	
						Thomas	
1895. Jan.	20	To CASH,		94	£15	,,	
						Perkin	
1895. Jan.	31	To CASH,		94	£100	6	
						James	
1895. Jan	4	To GENERAL STORES ACCOUNT, as per Sales Day Book,		101	£ ,,	19	
						Robert	
1895. Jan.	7	To INCIDENTAL RECEIPTS ACCOUNT, as per Sales Day Book,		101	£12	3	

White. Cr.

			Folio			
95. Jan.	5	By GENERAL STORES ACCOUNT, as per Purchase Day Book,	97	£1	4	11

& Co. Cr.

			Folio			
95. Jan.	15	By GENERAL STORES ACCOUNT, as per Purchase Day Book,	97	£104	,,	,,

Brown. Cr.

			Folio			
95. Jan.	17	By SUNDRIES ACCOUNT, as per Purchase Day Book,	97	£15	,,	,,

& Webb. Cr.

			Folio			
95. Jan.	31	By GENERAL STORES ACCOUNT, as per Purchase Day Book,	98	£100	6	,,

Thomson. Cr.

			Folio			
95. Jan.	10	By CASH,	93	£ ,,	19	5

Anderson. Cr.

			Folio			
95. Jan.	10	By CASH,	93	£7	,,	,,

𝔚ages 𝔖heets.

Form **6.**

Responsible Officer.

      The Wages Clerk. He should be under the close personal superintendence of both the General Manager and the Commercial Superintendent.

Foreman's Time Book.

      The Foremen of the departments **A** to **F** should each have a book into which the time of all their men is entered (see page 15), and on which the Wages Sheets are based.

      The **number of men** charged to the various departments in the Wages Sheets should be checked and agreed by the Accountant with the various departmental reports of work done from **A** to **F**, where the number of men employed are also enumerated.

      The **number of men** at work on Repairs and Renewals to Plant, which is done by the staff specially kept for repairing, and the apportionment of time to each particular part of the plant, should be clearly shewn in the Repairing Foreman's Book, so that the proper account can be charged with it. This **distribution** is shewn in Form **G**.

      It is often convenient to keep one or two labourers for doing general work, who may be moved about as ordered by the Manager.

      A note should be kept of the different jobs on which they have been engaged, and the proper department debited.

Entries.

      These are taken from the Foremen's time Books above referred to. Sometimes the Foreman also writes up the Wages Sheet, and the pay is calculated out by the Wages Clerk.

      If any deductions have to be made from the men's wages for Stores or other charges, a separate column must be provided on the Form for this purpose.

Salaries.

      The salaries of the following should be charged in their proper departments in the Wages Sheet :—

> **MINE SURVEYOR.**
> **MINE FOREMAN OR CAPTAIN.**
> **MILL SUPERINTENDENT.**
> **METALLURGIST.**
> **MECHANICAL ENGINEER.**

      The salaries of the following officials should be charged direct through the Cash Book to General Charges :—

> **GENERAL MANAGER.**
> **COMMERCIAL SUPERINTENDENT.**
> **ACCOUNTANT AND/OR CASHIER.**
> **ASSAYER.**
> **WAGES CLERKS.**
> **STORES CLERKS OR STOREKEEPERS.**

The Total of Wages to be Entered in the Journal (Form No. 4), page 105, and credited there to Sundry Workmen in the manner shewn.

Specimens (see pages 147 and 148).

The wages are paid weekly, fortnightly, or monthly, according to the custom of the country.

A copy is given of the Forms in common use in the Transvaal and in Australia.

It is usual in Australia to get the men to sign their names on the Wages Sheet when they receive their pay, payment being often made by cheque.

It will be observed that, in the corner of the Wages Sheet, a Summary is given of the expenditure under the sub-heads.

Wages Summary.

The above-mentioned Summaries made in the corner of each several Wages Sheet are gathered into one schedule in this form for incorporation in the General Expenditure Sheet (see pages 163 to 166). A specimen is to be found on pages 149 and 150.

Copies for the Head Office.

Copy of Wages Sheets to be forwarded monthly to the Head Office on the Form as arranged.

SPECIMEN of 𝔚𝔞𝔤𝔢𝔰 𝔖𝔥𝔢𝔢𝔱𝔰

..................Mine.   *This Sheet may be used for a single level or section of a Mine, as*

NAME.	NUMBER.	CLASS OF LABOUR.	WHERE EMPLOYED.	HOW EMPLOYED.	TOT
W. Griffiths,		Foreman,		Stoping, 14 / Driving, 8 / Tramming, 2	2.
F. Jones,		Blacksmith,		Stoping, 14 / Driving, 6 / Tramming, 4	2.
J. Johnson,		Miner,		Stoping, 23	2.
G. Watson,		,,		Driving, 21	2.
Natives, No.	501	Miner,	Stope No. 37,	Stoping, 24	2.
	502	,,	,, ,,	Stoping, 24	2.
	503	Labourer,		Tramming, 24	4.
	504	Miner,	No. 2 Level,	Driving, 9	2.
	505	,,	,, ,,	Driving, 24	2.
	506	Cook,		Driving, 12 / Stoping, 12	2.
	507	Labourer,		Tramming, 24	2.
	508 &c.	Miner, &c.	Stope No. 38,	Stoping, 24 &c.	2.

```
┌──────────────────────────┐
│        SUMMARY.          │
│ Mining—                  │
│  Stoping,  ... £120  4  6 │
│  Driving,  ...   26 17  4 │
│  Tramming, ...   15 10  3 │
│     &c.          &c.      │
│               ───────────│
│            £239 16  2     │
└──────────────────────────┘
```

..................Mine.   *This Sheet may be used for a single level or section of a Mine, a.*

NAME.	NUMBER.	CLASS OF LABOUR.	WHERE EMPLOYED.	HOW EMPLOYED.	TOT
Benson,	1	Miner,	Stope south from No. 8 Shaft over Level,	Stoping, 12	1
Jones,	2	,,		Stoping, 12	1
Williams,	3	,,	Driving south from No. 8 Shaft—Level,	Driving, 9	1
Harvey,	4	,,		Driving, 12	1
Lloyd,	5	,,	Sinking No.	Sinking, 12	1
Evans, &c.	6 &c.	,, &c.	Shaft (wet), &c.	Sinking, 12	1

```
┌──────────────────────────┐
│ Mining—  SUMMARY.        │
│  2 Stoping, ...   £      │
│  2 Driving, ...          │
│  2 Sinking, ...          │
│     &c.       ───────────│
│              £8  5        │
└──────────────────────────┘
```

147

Specimen.

arranged, and also for the different departments of the Reduction Works. February, 1897.

DAYS WORKED.																													RATE.	AMOUNT.		
3	4	5	6	7	8	9	10	11	12	13	14	15	16	17	18	19	20	21	22	23	24	25	26	27	28	29	30	31		£	s.	d.
/	/	/	/		/	/	/	/	/	/	/		/	/	/	/	/	/		/	/	/	/	/					£50 per mo.,	50	„	„
/	/	/	/		/	/	/	/	/	/	/		/	/	/	/	/	/		/	/	/	/	/					20/ per day,	24	„	„
/	/	/	/		/	/	/	/	/	/	/		/	/	/	/	/	/		/	/	/	/	/					18/4 „	21	1	8
/	/	/	/		/	/	/	/	/	/	/		/	/	/	/	/	/		/	/	/	/	/					16/8 „	17	10	„
																														£92	11	8
/	/	/	/		/	/	/	/	/	/	/		/	/	/	/	/	/		/	/	/	/	/					40/ per mo.,	2	„	„
/	/	/	/		/	/	/	/	/	/	/		/	/	/	/	/	/		/	/	/	/	/					35/ „	1	15	„
/	/	/	/		/	/	/	/	/	/	/		/	/	/	/	/	/		/	/	/	/	/					30/ „	1	10	„
															/	/	/	/	/		/	/	/	/	/				35/ „	„	13	„
/	/	/	/		/	/	/	/	/	/	/		/	/	/	/	/	/		/	/	/	/	/					32/6 „	1	12	6
/	/	/	/		/	/	/	/	/	/	/		/	/	/	/	/	/		/	/	/	/	/					37/6 „	1	17	6
/	/	/	/		/	/	/	/	/	/	/		/	/	/	/	/	/		/	/	/	/	/					30/ „	1	10	„
/	/	/	/		/	/	/	*&c.*	/	/	/		/	/	/	/	/	/		*&c.*	/	/	/	/					40/ „ *&c.*	2	*&c.*	„
																														£239	16	2

Date.....................................

.... Wages Clerk.

Specimen.

arranged, and also for the different departments of the Reduction Works. Ending 3rd March, 1897.

DAYS WORKED.											RATE.	AMOUNT.			RECEIVED PAYMENT.
20 S.	22 M.	23 T.	24 W.	25 Th.		26 F.	27 S.	28 M.	1 T.	2 W.	3 Th.		£	s.	d.	
		/	/	/		/	/	/	/	/	/	11/8	7	„	„	
/	/	/	/	/		/	/	/	/	/	/	11/8	7	„	„	
		/	/	/		/	/	/	/	/	/	11/8	5	5	„	
/	/	/	/	/		/	/	/	/	/	/	11/8	7	„	„	
/	/	/	/	/		/	/	/	/	/	/	13/4	8	„	„	
/	/	/	/	/		/	/	/	/	/	/	13/4	8	„	„	
		&c.				*&c.*						*&c.*	*&c.*			

> **Note.**
>
> The Forms on this page may be filled in by the Fore-man and handed in to the Office, the calculations being afterwards extended in the last column of the Office Staff.

Date,....................................

148

.... Wages Clerk.

For the Month

Form shewing Details of Work done.	ALLOCATION SCHEDULES giving CLASSIFICATION of WORK.	NATIVE WORKMEN.	OTHER WORKMEN.				TOTAL.		
				£	s.	d.	£	s.	d.
A	Prospecting—Surface,			...	...	...			
B	Prospecting—Underground,			36	11	11			
							36	11	11
C	Development—								
	Sinking,			...	...	...			
	Driving Levels,			5	14	"			
							5	14	...
C	Mining—								
	Sinking,			12	3	6			
	Driving Levels,			26	17	4			
	Stoping,			120	4	6			
	Tramming and Haulage to Surface,			15	10	3			
F	Power (Steam or otherwise),			...	...	...			
							174	15	
C	Transport to Mill—			40	19	"			
F	Power (Steam or otherwise),			...	...	...			
							40	19	
D	Milling and Crushing—			116	3	10			
F	Power (Steam or otherwise),			...	...	...			
							116	3	10
E	Cyaniding—			104	4	6			
	Sands Plant,			...	...	...			
	Slimes Plant,			...	...	...			
F	Power (Steam or otherwise),			...	...	...			
							104	4	6
	Office, Store, &c.—								
	Laboratory,			2	"	"			
	Office and Store,			4	"	"			
	Staff Quarters,			...	...	...			
	Stable,			3	"	"			
							9	"	"
	Forward,						£487	8	10

of *January, 1895.*   (*See Form* 6 *for details.*)

showing details of work done.		ALLOCATION SCHEDULES *giving* CLASSIFICATION *of* WORK.	NATIVE WORKMEN.	OTHER WORKMEN.			TOTAL.		
					£	s.	d.	£	s.	d.
G	C	**MAINTENANCE OF PLANT.**			Forward,			487	8	10
		MINING—								
		Pumping Gear,			,,	,,	,,			
		Rock Drills and Compressors,			,,	,,	,,			
		HAULAGE—								
		Hauling Gear,			15	,,	,,			
		Underground Tramway,			,,	,,	,,			
		Main Shaft,			,,	,,	,,			
		Houses over Hauling Engines,			6	1	2			
		TRANSPORT—								
		Maintenance of Tramways,			10	2	5			
	D	MILLING—								
		Mills, Rock-breakers, &c.,			15	4	2			
		Houses over Mills,			,,	,,	,,			
	E	CYANIDING—								
		Sands Plant,			22	1	2			
		Slimes Plant,			,,	,,	,,			
		Houses over Cyanide Plant,			7	6	10			
	F	POWER—								
		Pumping Engines and Boilers,			,,	,,	,,			
		Hauling Engines and Boilers,			,,	,,	,,			
		Hydraulic Power, including Mill Race,			,,	,,	,,			
		Mill Engines and Boilers,			,,	,,	,,			
		Dynamos, Motors, and Transformers,			,,	,,	,,			
		Electric Cable Lines,			,,	,,	,,			
		Switch Boards and Instruments,			,,	,,	,,			
		Oil Engines,			,,	,,	,,			
		OFFICE, STORE, &c.—								
		Laboratory,			,,	,,	,,			
		Office and Store,			,,	,,	,,			
		Staff Quarters,			,,	,,	,,			
		Stables,			,,	,,	,,			
								75	15	9

NOTE.—*The particulars of Maintenance are found in Form* G *when a special Maintenance Staff is kept, or in Forms* C, D, E, *and* F *when the Repairs are done by the Departmental Staffs.*

ERECTION OF NEW PLANT
The same order of the schedule of departments should be kept as used above for the Maintenance of Plant. The Form G *can be used when the erection of New Plant is being on.*

| | | | | | LEDGER ACCOUNT, | | | £663 | 4 | 7 |

Stores Ledger.

Form **7.**

Responsible Officer.—The Stores Clerk.

The Storekeeper should, by careful attention to the Stores Ledger, verify his stocks from time to time when these run low. A list of articles running out should be handed to the General Manager in time, so that he can get the stocks replaced if required.

Stores Ledger Balances.

A list of these to be forwarded to Head Office half-yearly, or periodically, as arranged.

Distribution of Stores.

The directions for the proper distribution and charging of stores to the different departments are to be found in the Stores Issued Book (Form **7a**), page 155.

> A Statement tabulated in any suitable form should be made up periodically, shewing the particulars of articles most in use, such as fuel, timber, wearing parts of machinery, tools, and like goods, and how they are distributed to the various subdivisions of the work.

Entries.

The weight, quantity, and value of all goods and supplies of every kind, machinery, tools, furniture, stationery, chemicals, &c., should be entered in the Stores Ledger under the respective accounts to which they belong. The entries for the DEBIT side are almost all obtained from the Purchase Day Book, and the total of the items so posted every month must also be posted to the DEBIT of the General Stores Account in the Mines Ledger.

The DELIVERED or CREDIT side may be most conveniently posted from the Stores Issued Book, the total of which is passed through the Sales Day Book, from which the corresponding CREDIT posting is obtained for the General Stores Account in the Mines Ledger.

Specimen.

See page 153.

Copies for the Head Office.

No copy of this book to be sent to the Head Office, as sufficient information is given in Stores Issued Book (Form **7a**) and in the Purchase Day Book.

SPACE RESERVED FOR MS. NOTES.

DRILL STEEL.

		RECEIVED.							ISSUED.				
Date.	Folio.	Quantity or Weight.	Rate.	Value.			Date.	Folio.	Quantity or Weight.	Rate.	Value.		
1895.		Qrs. Lbs.		£	s.	d.	1895.		Qrs. Lbs.		£	s.	d.
Jan.	1	STOCK,					Jan.	156	2 8½	5d.	1	12	3
,,		3 9	56}	2	2	,,							
	97	2 14		1	4	11							

SHOVELS.

1895.				£	s.	d.	1895.				£	s.	d.
Jan.	1	STOCK,					Jan.	156	6	3/9	1	2	6
		120	3/9	22	10	,,							

LIME.

1895.				£	s.	d.	1895.				£	s.	d.
Jan.	1	STOCK,					Jan.	101	1 Bag,	11/6	,,	11	6
		5 Bags,	11/6	2	17	6							

ENGINES.

1895.				£	s.	d.
Jan.		1 Winding,		695	6	,,
	97	Cost,		670	,,	,,
	98	Transport,		25	6	,,

DYNAMITE.

			RECEIVED.								ISSUED.					
	Folio.	Quantity or Weight.	Rate.	Value.			Date	Folio.	Quantity or Weight.	Rate.	Value.					
				£	s.	d.	1895.				£	s.	d.			
		STOCK, 50 Cases,	95/	237	10	,,	Jan.,	150	6 Packets,	9/	2	14	,,			

CRUCIBLES.

				£	s.	d.	1895.				£	s.	d.			
		STOCK, 24 Clay,	7d.	,,	14	,,	Jan.	101	10 Clay,	7d.	,,	5	10			

Note.

Arrangement of the Stores Ledger.

In practice, the pages should be larger than shewn in this Specimen, so that a large number of Accounts can be shewn at one opening.

Some skill can be shewn in the way in which the Accounts can be arranged in this book. Each Account should have a number of its own. These should be conveniently grouped together; for instance, the different picks might be one set of numbers, and the shovels another, and so on. Additional columns can be added if any further information is wanted.

Stocks.

These Accounts should be treated similarly to Ordinary Ledger Accounts, bringing down, periodically, the balance on hand, which in every case must of course be a debit balance representing the stock on hand.

Machinery.

Each piece of Machinery should have a separate Account of its own.

Index.

A complete index should be made of the Accounts in the Stores Ledger for easy reference.

THE STORES ISSUED OR STORES USED BOOK.

Form **7**a.

In this book is recorded the distribution of Stores referred to under the head of Stores Ledger, on page 151.

Responsible Officer.—The Stores Clerk.

Foreman's Order.

No stores are to be issued without a Foreman's Order (see Specimen on page 18). These orders should state the articles wanted, and the department or subdivision in which they are to be used. The orders should be kept conveniently on a file till the end of the month, when they should be sorted out and summarized—all picks together, all shovels together, and so on, so as to facilitate the making up of this book.

Entries.

This book is written up from the Foremen's Orders above referred to, and contains, in an analytical form, full details of all Stores issued under the departmental headings chargeable with them.

𝕾𝖙𝖔𝖗𝖊𝖘 𝕴𝖘𝖘𝖚𝖊𝖉 𝖔𝖗 𝖀𝖘𝖊𝖉 𝕭𝖔𝖔𝖐

Weights, Measures, and Quantities.

DESCRIPTION.	Rate.	MINING.				Transport to Mill.	Milling and Crushing.	Cyaniding.	
		Sinking.	Driving Levels.	Stoping.	Tramming to Surface.				
Rations—Mealies,	26/3 mul.	2 mds.	3¼ mds.	9¾ mds.	6¼ mds.				
Steel,	6d. lb.	48¼ lbs.	21 lbs.						
Picks,	3/ ea.			3					
Shovels,	3/9 ea.			6					
Hammers,	4½d. lb.			28 lbs.					
Hammer Handles,	4d. ea.			4					
Iron (Square),	4d. lb.				16 lbs.				
Timber, × ×	ft.	ft.	ft.	ft.					
Dynamite,	9/ pkt.		6 pkts.						
Fuse,	5/1 box.		1 box.						
Paraffin,	2/6 gal.	1 gal.	2 gals.	9 gals.	3 gals.				
Linseed Oil,	9d. bot.		3 bot.						
Anti-friction Grease,	4d. lb.				60 lbs.				
Lard Oil,	5/3 gal.				1 gal.				
Wheelbarrows,					:				
&c.,									
&c.,									

FOR GOLD MINING BUSINESS.

Postings.

From this book are obtained the postings for the DELIVERED or CREDITOR side of the Accounts in the Stores Ledger. The total of same is to be entered in the Sales Day Book, from which the corresponding CREDIT posting is obtained for the General Stores Account in the Mines Ledger.

Specimen.

A suitable form for this book is shewn at foot.

Copies for the Head Office.

A copy of "Stores Issued or Stores Used" book is to be sent monthly to the Head Office on the Form provided for the purpose.

Stores Summary.

This requires to be made up in a scheduled form suitable for incorporation in the General Expenditure Sheet (see pages 163 to 166).

A specimen is to be found overleaf on pages 157 to 160.

for the Month of January, 1895.

Amounts charged to Departments.

tal ntity.	Stores Ledger Folio.	Total Value.	MINING.				Transport to Mill.	Milling and Crushing.	Cyaniding.
			Sinking.	Driving Levels.	Stoping.	Tramming to Surface.			
		£ s. d.	£ s. d.	£ s. d.	£ s. d.	£ s. d.			
nds.	×	28 18 1	2 12 6	4 18 10	12 19 6	8 7 3			
lbs.	153	1 12 3	1 1 9	„ 10 6					
	×	„ 9 „			„ 9 „				
	153	1 2 6			1 2 6				
bs.	×	„ 10 6			„ 10 6				
	×	„ 1 4			„ 1 4				
s.	×	„ 5 3				„ 5 3			
	×	7 18 1	2 5 7	2 10 „	„ 3 2 6				
ets.	154	2 14 „		2 14 „					
or.	×	„ 5 1		„ 5 1					
ds.	×	1 17 4	„ 2 6	„ 5 „	1 2 4	„ 7 6			
ots.	×	„ 2 3		„ 2 3					
s.	×	1 „ „				1 „ „			
nl.	×	„ 5 3				„ 5 3			
	×	2 10							

.....Stores Clerk.

156

For the Month

Form shewing Details of Work done.	ALLOCATION SCHEDULES giving CLASSIFICATION of WORK.	RATIONS.			TOOLS & MOVABLE PLANT.			TIMBER.			EXPLOSIVES.			OILS, &c., FOR LIGHTING & LUBRICATING			WEARING PART OF MACHINERY		
		£	s.	d.	£	s.	d.	£	s.	d.	£	s.	d.	£	s.	d.	£	s.	d.
A	Prospecting—Surface,																		
B	Prospecting—Underground,	2	17	3	1	15	4	1	10	,,	,,	10	,,	,,	15	,,	1	5	
C	Development—																		
	Sinking,																		
	Driving Levels,	2	10	,,	,,	10	3												
C	Mining—																		
	Sinking,	2	12	6	1	1	9	2	5	7				,,	2	6			
	Driving Levels,	4	18	10	,,	10	6	2	19	,,	2	19	1	,,	7	3			
	Stoping,	12	19	6	2	3	4	3	2	6				1	2	4			
	Tramming & Haulage to Surface,	8	7	3	,,	5	3							1	12	9	2	10	,,
F	Power (Steam or otherwise),																		
C	Transport to Mill—	8	8	11	2	7	1							2	,,	10			
F	Power (Steam or otherwise),																		
D	Milling and Crushing—	17	2	8	4	19	2							5	8	1			
F	Power (Steam or otherwise),																		
E	Cyaniding—Sands Plant,	18	1	10	1	5	4							1	4	3			
	Slimes Plant,																		
F	Power (Steam or otherwise)																		
	Office, Store, &c.—																		
	Laboratory,	,,	15	,,	7	1	3							,,	7	3			
	Office and Store,	1	10	,,	...	...	...							,,	15	,,	1	,,	,,
	Staff Quarters,																		
	Stable,	,,	15	,,	,,	6	,,							,,	5	7			
	Total		18	9				£9	8	1	£3	9	1	£14	..	10	£4	15	,,

of January, 1895.   (See Form **7a** for details).

FUEL.	MERCURY.			CYANIDE.			CHEMICALS & LABORATORY ACCESSORIES.			SUNDRIES.									TOTAL.		
	£	s.	d.	£	s.	d.	£	s.	d.	£	s.	d.				£	s.	d.	£	s.	d.
																...	...	...	8	12	7
																...	...	...	3	„	3
																6	2	4			
																11	5	8			
																19	7	8			
																12	16	3			
																...	...	...	49	10	11
																12	16	10			
																...	...	...	12	16	10
	7	7	„													34	16	11			
																...	...	...	34	16	11
				114	16	„	5	„	„							139	19	5			
																...	...	...	139	19	5
							8	14	7							16	18	1			
										5	„	„				6	5	„			
																1	6	7			
																			24	9	8
...	...	...	£7	7	„	£114	16		£13	14	7	5	„	„	...	...	...	£273	6	7

Form shewing Details of Work done.		ALLOCATION SCHEDULES giving CLASSIFICATION of WORK.	RATIONS.			TOOLS & MOVABLE PLANT.			TIMBER.			EXPLOSIVES.			OILS, &c., FOR LIGHTING & LUBRICATING			WEARING PART OF MACHINERY	
			£	s.	d.	£	s.	d	£	s.	d.	£	s.	d.	£	s.	d.	£	s.
		Forward,	80	18	9	22	8	5	9	8	1	3	9	1	14	,,	10	4	15
		MAINTENANCE OF PLANT.																	
G	C	MINING—																	
		Pumping Gear,																	
		Rock Drills and Compressors,																	
		HAULAGE—																	
		Hauling Gear,	,,	15	n	,,	8	6											
		Underground Tramway,																	
		Main Shaft,																	
		Houses over Hauling Engines,	,,	5	6														
		TRANSPORT—																	
		Maintenance of Tramways,	3	1	7	,,	2	6										7	1
	D	MILLING—																	
		Mills, Rock-breakers, &c.,	1	7	6	1	10	,,											
		Houses over Mills,																	
	E	CYANIDING—																	
		Sands Plant,	3	10	4	,,	15	4	18	7	6								
		Slimes Plant,																	
		Houses over Cyanide Plant,	,,	8	5														
	F	POWER—																	
		Pumping Engines and Boilers,																	
		Hauling Engines and Boilers,																	
		Hydraulic Power, including Mill Race,																	
		Mill Engines and Boilers,																	
		Dynamos, Motors, and Transformers,																	
		Electric Cable Lines,																	
		Switch Boards and Instruments,																	
		Oil Engines, &c																	
		OFFICE, STORE, &c.,																	
		Laboratory,																	
		Office and Store,																	
		Staff Quarters,																	
		Stables,																	
		(See Note on Page 150.)																	
		ERECTION OF NEW PLANT (See Note on page 150.)																	
			89	2	1	£24	19	7	27	15	7	3	9	1	14	,,	10	£11	16

of January, 1895. (See Form 7a for details).

FUEL.			MERCURY.			CYANIDE.			CHEMICALS & LABORATORY ACCESSORIES.			SUNDRIES.									TOTAL.		
£	s.	d.	£	s.	d.	£	s.	d.	£	s.	d.	£	s.	d.				£	s.	d.	£	s.	d.
...	...	...	7	7	„	114	10	„	13	14	7	3	„	„	...	...	...				273	6	7
												1	12	9				2	16	3			
																		„	5	6			
																		9	5	8			
24	19	2										4	„	„				31	16	8			
												2	„	„				24	13	2			
												„	17	3				1	„	8			
																		69	17	11			

| 24 | 19 | 2 | £7 | | | 114 | | | | | | | | | | ... | | As per LEDGER ACCOUNT £342 | 4 | 6 |

General Expenditure Sheet.

Form **8.**

Responsible Officers.—The General Manager, the Commercial Superintendent, and the Accountant.

Entries.

The GENERAL EXPENDITURE SHEET combines in one schedule the total outgoings for the month, arranged under their respective departmental headings, and classified in columns corresponding to the four Ledger Accounts.

The figures in the WAGES Column are taken from the WAGES SUMMARY, pages 149, 150.

,,	STORES ,, ,,	STORES SUMMARY, pages 157 to 160.
,,	GENERAL CHARGES, ,,	LEDGER ACCOUNT, &c., pp. 135, 136.
,,	SUNDRIES, ,,	LEDGER ACCOUNT, pages 137, 138.

The figures of quantities are taken as follows :—

A, SURFACE PROSPECTING BOOK, pages 45 and 46.

B, UNDERGROUND PROSPECTING BOOK, pages 51 and 52, or 55 and 56.

C, MINING AND ORE TRANSPORT REPORT BOOK, pages 55 and 56.

D, MILLING AND CRUSHING REPORT BOOK, pages 63 and 64.

E, CYANIDING REPORT BOOK, pages 67 and 68.

F, POWER REPORT BOOK, pages 75 and 76.

G, MAINTENANCE OF PLANT BOOK, pages 87 and 88.

> *Note.*—There are also the items of maintenance of Plant carried out by the Departments **C, D, E,** and **F.** The total of the Maintenance Account should be distributed at the end of the year according to the Expenditure Schedules.

Specimen.

See pages 163 to 166.

Copies for the Head Office.

Copy of the General Expenditure Sheet to be forwarded monthly to the Head Office on the Form provided for the purpose.

SPACE RESERVED FOR MS. NOTES.

Total Expenditure—namely, Wages, Stores Issued, General

Form showing Details of Work done.	WORK DONE.	ALLOCATION SCHEDULES giving CLASSIFICATION of WORK.	WAGES, as per Form 6.			
			Native Workmen.	Other Workmen.	Total.	
			£ s. d.	£ s. d.	£	s. d.
A		Prospecting—Surface,			...	... ...
B		Prospecting—Underground,			36	11 11
C		Development—				
		Sinking,			...	... ...
		Driving Levels,			5	14
C		Mining—				
	75 ft.,	Sinking,			12	3
	127 ,,	Driving Levels,			26	17 4
	680 tons,	Stoping,			120	4
	689 ,,	Tramming and Haulage to Surface,			15	10
F		Power (Steam or otherwise),			...	... ...
C	750 tons,	Transport to Mill—			40	19
F		Power (Steam or otherwise),			...	... ...
D	1000 tons,	Milling and Crushing—			116	8 10
F		Power (Steam or otherwise),			...	... ...
E	850 tons,	Cyaniding—Sands Plant,			104	4
		Slimes Plant,			...	... ...
F		Power (Steam or otherwise),			...	... ...
		Office, Store, &c.—				
		Laboratory,			2	,, ,,
		Office and Store,			4	,, ,,
		Staff Quarters,			...	... ...
		Stable,			3	,, ,,
		Salaries,				
		Other Charges,				
		Forward,			£487	8 10

Charges, and Sundries, *for the Month of January, 1895.*

STORES. as per Form 7a.			GENERAL CHARGES.			SUNDRIES.			TOTAL.			REMARKS.
£	s.	d.	£	s.	d.	£	s.	d.	£	s.	d.	
...	...	...							...	...	...	
8	12	7							45	4	6	Development Account. *See Note on Development, page 126.*
...	...	...							...	...	...	
3	»	9							8	14	3	
6	2	4							18	5	10	
11	5	8							38	3	»	
19	7	8				15	»	»	154	12	2	
12	15	4							28	5	6	
...	...	...							...	...	...	
12	16	10							53	15	10	
..	...	...							...	...	...	
34	16	11							151	..	9	
..	...	...							...	...	...	
31	19	5							244	7	11	
..	...	...							...	...	...	
16	18	1							18	18	1	
6	5	»							10	5	»	
..	...	...							...	...	...	
1	6	7							4	6	7	
			8d	6	8				8d	6	8	
			83	1	10				83	1	10	
73	6	7	£166	8	6	£15	»	»	£942	3	11	

> ### Note.
>
> **Castings.**
>
> The figures in this return may be cast up in departments, as required, so long as the grand totals are brought out at the end, and are in agreement with the corresponding four Ledger Accounts for the month—namely,
>
> **Wages Account,**
> **Stores Used Account,**
> **General Charges Account,**
> **Sundries Account.**
>
> **General Charges and Sundries.**
>
> An Abstract of these, so arranged as to exhibit generally all information necessary for the Head Office, should form one of the Returns, but a specimen of same has not been thought necessary to be given here.

SPECIMEN *of* General Expenditure Sheet

Total Expenditure—namely, Wages, Stores Issued, General

Form showing Details of Work done.	ALLOCATION SCHEDULES giving CLASSIFICATION of WORK	WAGES, as per Form 6.						
		Native Workmen.	Other Workmen.			Total.		
			£	s.	d.	£	s.	d.
	Forward,					487	8	10
	MAINTENANCE OF PLANT.							
G C	MINING—							
	Pumping Gear,							
	Rock Drills and Compressors,							
	HAULAGE—							
	Hauling Gear,					15		
	Underground Tramway,							
	Main Shaft,							
	Houses over Hauling Engines					6	1	
	TRANSPORT—							
	Maintenance of Tramways,					10	2	
D	MILLING—							
	Mills, Rock-breakers, &c.,					15	4	
	Houses over Mills,							
E	CYANIDING—							
	Sands Plant,					22	1	
	Slimes Plant,							
	Houses over Cyanide Plant,					7	6	10
F	POWER—							
	Pumping Engines and Boilers,							
	Hauling Engines and Boilers,							
	Hydraulic Power, including Mill Race,							
	Mill Engines and Boilers,							
	Dynamos, Motors, and Transformers,							
	Electric Cable Lines,							
	Switch Boards and Instruments,							
	Oil Engines,							
	OFFICE, STORE, &c.—							
	Laboratory,							
	Office and Store,							
	Staff Quarters,							
	Stables,							
	(See Note on page 150.)	TOTALS as per LEDGER A/CS.,				£563	4	7
	ERECTION OF NEW PLANT.							
	(See Note on page 170.)							
		TOTALS as per LEDGER A/CS.,				...	...	...

Charges, and Sundries, *for the Month of January, 1895.*

STORES. as per Form 7a.			GENERAL CHARGES.			SUNDRIES.			TOTAL.			REMARKS.
£	s.	d.	£	s.	d.	£	s.	d.	£	s.	d.	
773	6	7	166	8	6	15	,,	,,	942	3	11	
2	16	3							17	16	8	
,,	5	6							6	6	8	
9	5	8							19	8	1	
31	16	8							47	,,	10	
23	13	2							35	14	4	
1	,,	8							8	7	6	
743	4	6	£166	8	6	£15	,,	,,	£1087	17	7	

Date,..........................

...............................*Commercial Superintendent.*

..................................*General Manager.*

TOTAL DEBIT to General Working Account.

TOTAL DEBIT to Erection of New Plant Account.

.

MONTHLY CABLEGRAM BOOK.

Form **8**a.

Responsible Officer.—The Commercial Superintendent.

Entries.—*The General Expenditure Sheet.*

Head Office.

The following are notes for guidance in despatching Cablegrams to the Head Office:—

In cases of work under development, or the erection of new works where no crushing is going on, the monthly telegram should be sent giving the total expenditure for the month. The code word for this telegram should be specifically arranged.

In cases of development, new works, and crushings going on, it must be observed that the working Expenses and Expenditure on New Plant are kept separate.

The Working Expenses, however, should include repairs or renewal of plant, Expenditure on Plant being cost and erection of new plant only.

As only one code word, representing quantity or amount, is to be used for each line, it is necessary always to send the messages in the same order as printed.

Presuming that no ore had been treated at the Mill, the second word in the message would be " Nil," which would be understood as applying to both the " Ore Crushed " and "Bullion Recovered."

Should there be occasion to give any further information in the monthly telegram, it must always come at the end, after the regular information (as printed) has been given.

This book should have interleaved perforated duplicates to be filled up by using carbon paper. They are then to be posted to the Head Office by first mail after the despatch of the cablegram to which they refer.

Specimen.

On the other side is a Specimen of a Cablegram.

As an example, in telegraphing a monthly return, the actual Code message is presumed to be as printed in red in the first column.

RESULTS OF THE MINES OPERATIONS

For the Month of .... 190.......

CODE WORD.	FOR		QUANTITY AND AMOUNT.
Votice.	**Mining,**	*Ore mined,*	*2,500 tons.*
Votagione,	**Milling,**	*Ore crushed,*	*2,300 tons.*
Unassisted.	**Do.,**	*Bullion recovered,*	*1,700 ozs.*
Vosklenrig.	**Cyaniding,**	*Ore, &c., treated,*	*1,800 tons.*
Unurtig,	**Do.,**	*Bullion recovered,*	*1,450 ozs.*
Unwrought,	**Estimated Value,**	*Total Bullion,*	*£9,100*
Unterburgt.	**Mining, Milling, and Cyaniding,** (including Repairs and General Charges,)	*Expenses,*	*£4,000*
Untastbar,	**Plant and other**	*Expenditure,*	*£240*

The PROGRESSIVE SUMMARY of the GENERAL EXPENDITURE SHEETS.

Form **8**b.

Responsible Officer.—The Accountant.

Entries.

The various headings of the Expenditure Sheet Schedules in form **8** may, for all practical purposes, be looked upon as so many subsidiary DEPARTMENTAL LEDGER ACCOUNTS, the figures appearing in the outer column being, as it were, the monthly postings. Some form of Summary Book therefore is required, in order to provide for the scheduling of these figures in such a manner as to bring out the accumulating figures throughout the year. This may be done in any convenient form, either by having the Column of Schedules vertical, and the months shown at the top of each column as on opposite page, or by having the Dates vertical, and the Schedule designation at the top of the column, as can be easily designed.

A Summary of this kind is of course open to considerable variations, according to amount of detail wanted. It may consist of the figures in the outer column only, or it may be preceded by summaries of the figures in say the Wages and Stores Issued columns respectively; in which case the book should be divided into three parts accordingly, but the form of ruling should be the same for each part.

Another form of Summary, and one that may commend itself to some Companies, would be to condense the figures and summarize them under the *principal headings only;* in which case the summary would also, as above, consist either of the total figures only, or of the Wages and Stores in separate parts.

In any case, the Expenditure Sheet Schedules (Form **8**) must be cast up according to the totals required.

Copies for the Head Office.

No copy of this book is sent to the Head Office monthly, but results can be sent on if required.

When periodically required for the Head Office, the progressive totals for three months, six months, or a year, can be filled in on one of the Monthly Expenditure Sheet Forms.

FOR GOLD MINING BUSINESS.

Specimen.

NOTE.—*The figures in black ink represent the monthly expenditure taken from the Expenditure Schedules in No.* **8,** *those in red being the progressive totals.*

DEPARTMENTS.	JANUARY.	FEBRUARY.	MARCH.	&c.
	£ s. d.	£ s. d.	£ s. d.	
Prospecting—*Surface,*	... ...	... ...	... ...	
Prospecting—*Underground,*	45 4 6	37 10 0	41 2 6	&c.
	... ...	82 14 6	123 17 0	&c.
Development—				
Sinking,	... ...	... ...	... ...	
Driving Levels,	8 14 3	10 16 9	7 5 2	&c.
	... ...	19 11 0	26 16 2	&c.
Mining—				
Sinking,	18 5 10	16 4 2	20 1 2	
Driving Levels,	38 3 0	31 7 9	40 2 4	
Stoping,	154 12 2	140 12 8	183 5 10	
Tramming and Haulage to				&c.
Surface,	28 5 6	22 5 6	37 14 9	
Power (Steam or otherwise),	... ...	... ...	... ...	
	... ...	503 12 5	855 16 8	&c.
Transport to Mill—	53 15 10	50 14 2	65 13 3	&c.
Power (Steam or otherwise),	... ...	... ...	... ...	
	... ...	104 10 0	170 3 5	&c.
&c.				

NOTE.—*The progressive totals only may be used if preferred, so as to shorten the summarising; in which*

THE CLASSIFICATION OF MINING COSTS.

In order to shew the general applicability of the Schedules set out in the preceding pages, the following table has been drawn up, giving a comparison of the heads of classification appearing in the published accounts of three important Mines in the Transvaal, with those adopted in the Specimen Forms contained in this book :—

SPECIMEN SCHEDULE (as on pages 163 and 164).	MINE No. 1.	MINE No. 2.	MINE No. 3.
DEVELOPMENT.	DEVELOPMENT.	DEVELOPMENT.	DEVELOPMENT.
MINING. *Sinking. Driving Levels, includes Rising and Sinking Winzes. Stoping. Tramming in Mine & Haulage to Surface. Power, Steam or otherwise.*	MINING. *Timbering. Driving, Rising, and Sinking Winzes. Stoping. Tramming in Mine. Winding or Haulage to Surface. Pumping.*	MINING.	MINING.
TRANSPORT TO MILL. *Power, Steam or otherwise.*	TRANSPORT TO MILL.	TRANSPORT TO MILL.	TRANSPORT TO MILL.
MILLING & CRUSHING. *Power, Steam or otherwise.*	MILLING.	MILLING. *Water.*	MILLING.
CYANIDING. *Sands, Slimes, Power, Steam or otherwise.*	CYANIDING.	CYANIDING.	CYANIDING.
CONCENTRATES (*if any*).	*None.*	CONCENTRATES. *Vanners. Chlorination.*	*None.*
POWER (*as above distributed*).	(*Included in Milling.*)	FUEL.	(*Included in Milling.*)
GENERAL CHARGES.	GENERAL CHARGES.	GENERAL CHARGES.	GENERAL CHARGES. ENGINEERS' DEPT. ASSAY DEPT.

It cannot always, however, be clearly discerned in these published accounts where one department begins and another ends; or what sub-heads have been included in each department, as can be done in the Rules here set forth; the units of costs, therefore, cannot be accurately compared till some uniformity of definition of each department is established.

A comparative table, giving details of the costs of working of the more important Mines of the Rand, is to be found in page 264, Hatch & Chalmers' "Mines of the Rand."

The remarks to that table illustrate the difference of practice which prevails in distributing charges to the different departments.

The proper assessment or distribution of the expenditure requires the careful attention of all persons connected with mining. It is recommended to the various Chambers of Mines that such distribution of costs should form a subject for united action, so that definite rules for the general acceptance may be formulated.

GOLD STATEMENTS.

Introduction.

Having dealt in the previous parts of the book with the Organization of the Staff, the Departmental Records, and the Account Books, it now remains to show how the final results obtained from the treatment of the Ore are set out; and in this connection the Diagram given on page 40 should be referred to.

The London transactions with the Gold are explained, and it is believed that the explanation may be of general interest.

GOLD STATEMENT,
Shewing Gold contained in Ore, Residues, and Bullion.

Form **9.**

Responsible Officers.—The General Manager, the Commercial Superintendent, and the Accountant.

Entries.

The total tonnage delivered to be treated should be taken from   Report **C.**
The tonnage milled in Stamp Battery should be taken from   ,, **D.**
The tonnage treated in the Cyanide Vats as sands and/or slimes
    should be taken from   ,, **E.**
The weight of Gold Bullion is taken from the Assay Certificate (see page 37).

The ENTRIES should shew the Gold Contents of FINE GOLD in the Ore by the Assay Certificate of the sample of Ore taken when being filled into the mill.

In practice it is found the filling assay is usually slightly under the mine assay. The mine assay is more difficult to obtain accurately than the filling assay; which latter is taken from the Ore after it has passed through the stone-breaker, and consequently the reduced bulk sample is more representative of the whole.

No stocks of Ore on hand are shewn here, as the Ore not filled into the mill remains at the credit of the Working Account at cost price (see page 121).

The ENTRIES also shew the weight and assay of the Bullion and the Gold produced in FINE GOLD.

The differences shew the loss in process, and the Gold left in the residues unextracted.

It should be clearly stated whether the tons are given as 2240 or 2000 lbs.; and this remark applies to tonnage weights throughout the whole of the accounts.

The assays of Ore and Bullion produced are taken from the Assay Certificate (see page 37).

If the Ore contains an appreciable quantity of Silver, provision should be made for shewing it fully in the Statement.

Specimens.—See pages 179 and 180.

Copies for the Head Office.

As all the particulars required for making up the GOLD STATEMENT are found in the various forms sent monthly to the Head Office, it need only be made up at the mines and sent to the Head Office, quarterly, half-yearly, or yearly, as may be required.

SHIPMENTS TO LONDON.

INSURANCE.—All Gold Bullion shipped from the mine should be covered by insurance against all risks, from the mill to its final destination in London, or to the local mint.

LONDON WEIGHTS AND ASSAYS.—The results obtained in London by the weighing and assaying done there may differ from the figures obtained at the mine. As a rule the differences are not great; but they should be observed, and noted, and advised back from London to the mine.

LONDON TRANSACTIONS IN GOLD.

Bullion Sales.

All Gold Bullion sent to London is consigned to the care of the Bank of England. A bullion broker should be employed to act for the importing Company, and the bill of Lading should be sent to him. The broker presents the Bill of Lading to the Bullion Office of the Bank of England, and on payment of freight and 1/9 per package of Bullion (the Bank charge for receiving the Bullion), can obtain his consignment of Gold.

The broker delivers the Bullion to one of the melters to the Bank, and it is his duty to see the Bullion weighed, melted, re-weighed, and delivered to the refiner to whom it may be sold.

Pieces of the Bullion, after melting, are sent to an assayer to the Bank of England for assay, and account sales (see page 177) are prepared on the basis of his results.

The Gold is paid for on the basis of the price of the market quotation for standard Gold, the Silver is paid for on the price of Fine Silver, both ruling on the day of sale. Certain charges are made for melting, refining, and assaying, and a reduction is made for some of the Gold produced by the cyanide process—the latter being always more or less impure, owing to being contaminated with zinc and lead, in varying proportions, according to the purity of the zinc used at the mine, and the subsequent more or less complete elimination of the zinc from the Gold mud.

Weighing.

The account sales shew the weight of the Bullion before and after melting, the latter being the basis of sale price.

Assaying.

The assay must be made by an assayer to the Bank of England, who gives a certificate of his assays in Fine Gold and Silver, to the 5/10,000th part for the former, and to the 1/1,000th part for the latter.

Cost of Melting and Assaying.

The charge is ¼d. per oz. of Bullion for melting, and 4/ per bar for assaying, except in the case of Cyanide Bars, when two distinct assays of each bar must be made—the fee being, consequently, 8/ per bar.

Refining.

The charge for this is 2¾d. per oz. of Bullion after melting.

Price.

The Bank of England price for Gold is £3 17s. 9d. per oz. of Standard Gold (22 carat or 916·6 fine); but the market price may be more if the demand for Gold be great. The assay shews the Fine Gold contained per 1000 parts of the bar, and by adding $\frac{1}{11}$th of the total Fine Gold contents in ozs. the total ozs. of Standard Gold is found. In the example given below, 500 ozs. of Bullion, assaying 800/1000 Fine Gold, becomes 400 ozs. Fine Gold; add $\frac{1}{11}$th, and the total Standard Gold contents is 436·363.

An allowance is made for the Silver according to the current market price of Fine Silver, which is, of course, higher than the more usually quoted price of Standard Silver (925/1000 fine).

Extra Deduction for Base Bullion (Cyanide Gold).

This Bullion being frequently very impure, a special deduction is made for the extra cost of refining, varying with the fineness shewn by the assay. The present rate of deduction is as follows :—

700 to 800 Fine	...	...	...	3 per 1000.
Below 700 Fine	...	...	...	4 „

The mean of two separate assay pieces of the metal is taken as definitive of the Fine Gold contents per 1000 parts. From this figure is deducted the above allowances, according to the fineness. In the example given on following page it is assumed that one assay shewed 751 and the other assay 749 per 1000—the mean being 750 to 1.

GOLD STATEMENTS.

ACCOUNT SALES.

Ordinary Bar Gold.

	Oz.			Assay.				
After melting,	500·000		Gold,	800·0				
			Silver,	150·0				

	Oz.	Oz.			£	s.	d.
Fine Gold,	400·000 =	436·363	Standard at 77/11,		£1699	19	11
Fine Silver,	75·000		at 26¾d.,		8	7	2

					£1708	7	1

Less—

Melting,	£ „ 16	6
Assay,	„ 4 „	
Refining,	5 14	7

			6	9	1

		£1701	18	0

London, 30th May, 1903.   Basis—Standard Gold, 77/11 per oz.

Note.

The above price, 77/11, is made up of the Bank of England price of 77/9 per oz. for Standard Gold, and the market premium of 2d. per oz. on the day of sale.

Cyanide Bar Gold.

	Oz.			Assays.		Mean.	Less 3/1000.
After melting,	500·000		Gold,	751·0	749·0	750·0	747·0
			Silver,	149·0	151·0	150·0	

	Oz.	Oz.			£	s.	d.
Fine Gold,	373·500 =	407·454	Standard at 77/11,		£1587	7	6
Fine Silver,	75·000		at 26¾d.,		8	7	2

				£1595	14	8

Less—

Melting,	£ „ 16	6
Assays,	„ 8 „	
Refining,	5 14	7

			6	19	1

		£1589	1	7

London, 30th May, 1903.   Basis—Standard Gold, 77/11 per oz.

Note.

The above price of 77/11 is made up of the Bank of England price of 77/9 per oz. for Standard Gold, and a market premium of 2d. per oz. on the day of sale.

ON SAMPLING AND ASSAYING BULLION.

In the case of ordinary Bullion, one Sample is taken of each bar, the assay piece being cut off one end of the bar ; in the case of Cyanide Gold the metal, while molten, is "dipped" twice for each bar, thus making two assays instead of one ; the mean of the two assays is taken as a settlement of the fineness. The assay of each "dip" is made in triplicate.

PRIMARY TREATMENT—MILLING AND AMALGAMATION.

1906. Month.	Ore filled into Mill.					Extracted per Ton as shewn by Assay. Dwts.	Gold Contents.			Actual Recovery.			% of Contents of Ore Milled.
	Gross Weight Tons.	Moisture. %	Dry Weight Tons.	Average Assay, per Ton. Dwts.	Average Assay, per Ton. Dwts.		In Charge. Dwts.	In Tailings. Dwts.	Estimated Yield. Fine Ounces.	BULLION. Ounces.	Fineness.	FINE GOLD. Ounces.	
Jan.,	1,307	5	1,242	14·7	4·4	10·3	18,257	5,465	639·6	833·8	768	640·3	70
Feb.,	1,250	5	1,188	13·	3·2	9·8	15,444	3,802	582·1	796·4	739·4	588·9	76·4
Mar.,	1,300	5	1,235	12·8	3·8	9·	15,808	4,693	555·8	681·9	761·7	519·4	65·7
Apr.,	1,660	5	1,577	10·26	3·53	6·83	16,180	5,330	542·5	759·3	748·7	564·7	68·8
May,	2,100	5	1,995	10·4	2·6	7·8	20,748	5,187	778·	1,009·4	776·5	783·8	75·5
June,	2,090	5	1,986	12·36	3·2	9·16	24,547	6,355	909·6	1,169·	778·9	910·6	74·2
July,	2,250	5	2,138	11·5	2·85	8·65	24,587	6,093	924·7	1,194·	770	919	74·7
Aug.,	2,030	5	1,928	11·22	3·22	8·	21,632	6,208	771·2	1,025·	750	768·7	71·1
Sept.,	2,140	5	2,033	10·55	3·49	7·06	21,448	7,095	717·7	965·	740	714·	66·6
Oct.,	2,275	5	2,162	11·21	3·16	8·05	24,236	6,832	870·2	1,130·	760	858·8	79·9
Nov.,	2,200	5	2,090	10·81	3·1	7·71	22,598	6,479	805·7	1,128·	709·9	801·8	71·
Dec.,	2,225	5	2,113	10·44	3·15	7·29	22,960	6,656	770·2	1,010·	770	777·7	70·5
...	...		1,687	11·41	3·237	8·177	247,540	70,195	8,867·3	11,701·5	756	8,847·25	71·5

Summary.

PRIMARY TREATMENT—   Dwts.   Percentages

    Actual yield Fine Gold by Amalgamation,   176,955   71·5

SECONDARY TREATMENT—

    Actual yield Fine Gold by Cyanide from Sands,   25,800   10·4

      „   „   „   Slimes,   9,529   3·85

      „   „   from Concentrates,   8,800   3·5

      „   „   „ Slags, &c.,   480   ·2

            Total Gold Recovered = 221,564   89·45 %

    Gold left in Residues,   15,944   6·55

    Gold lost in Process,   10,032   4·

      Total Gold in Original Ore treated = 247,540   100 %

1902.

SECONDARY TREATMENT—CYANIDING SANDS TAILINGS.

Sands Charged into Vats.	Residues.			Gold Contents.			Actual Recovery.				
Tons Dry Weight.	Average Assay. Dwts.	Average Assay. Dwts.	Extracted per Ton as shewn by Assay. Dwts.	In Charge. Dwts.	In Residues. Dwts.	Estimated Yield. Fine Ounces.	BULLION. Ounces.	Fineness.	FINE GOLD. Ounces.	% of Contents of Sands.	% of Contents of Original Ore Milled.
912	3·05	·76	2·29	2,782	693	104·45	257·5	404	104·08	75	11·69
900	2·68	·75	1·93	2,412	675	86·85	193·	450	86·85	72	11·25
980	3·13	·70	2·43	3,067	686	119·05	242·8	474	114·98	75	14·55
1,176	2·47	·55	1·92	2,905	647	112·9	302·8	350	105·98	72·9	13·1
1,637	1·82	·56	1·26	2,979	916	103·15	269·5	365	98·37	66	9·3
1,584	2·39	·77	1·62	3,786	1,220	128·3	210·1	594	124·79	65·9	10·16
1,636	2·19	·78	1·41	3,583	1,277	115·3	227·5	500·5	113·7	63·5	9·26
1,500	2·25	·81	1·44	3,374	1,215	108	233·75	444	103·78	61·5	9·6
1,496	2·2	·68	1·52	3,291	1,017	113·7	263·6	424	111·8	67·9	10·8
1,530	2·07	·75	1·32	3,169	1,148	101·05	286	351	100·30	63·3	10·28
1,539	2·41	·7	1·71	3,687	1,071	130·3	197·3	463	125·35	68·	10·13
1,530	2·1	·72	1·38	3,213	1,102	105·55	242·8	412	100·02	62·2	9·07
16,411	2·34	·71	1·62	38,249	11,667	1,329·1	...	...	1,290·04	62·4	10·4	Sands Treatment Totals.
4,830	8·68	·6	2·42	14,845	2,957	795·3	...	...	479·47	65·2	5·85	Slimes Treatment Totals.
67	160	·39	149	10,719	1,340	509	...	...	430	82	3·5	Concentrates Treatment Totals.
...	...	...	...	...	...	...	...	...	25	...	·2	Slags, &c.
21,308	2·99	·674	2·23	63,812	15,944	2,603·4	...	...	2,230·28	...	17·95	Totals from Secondary Treatment.

𝔑ote.

Only the Annual figures for Slimes and Concentrates are given above
to save space, but in actual practice the Monthly figures would be
shewn, as in the case of the Sands.

The actual may some months exceed the estimated yield according
to the way the Extractor boxes are cleaned up, but usually this will
right itself on an average of two or three months. The gold left in the
Extractor boxes should be carefully estimated at the end of each year,
and any difference from the previous year debited or credited, as the
case may be, to the process in the Annual Summary.

....General Manager.

....Commercial Superintendent.

SPACE RESERVED FOR MS. NOTES.

PROFIT AND LOSS OF GOLD MINING.

ANCIENT AND MODERN.

INTRODUCTION.

This chapter is written from a commercial and industrial stand-point. It is intended to stimulate enquiry into what makes gold-mining profitable by the organized scientific methods of to-day. It is chiefly a compilation of facts from sources of information which the compiler has found advantageous to himself in forming correct estimates of the true proportion and scope of the gold-mining business as an industry.

It starts with brief mention of the gold-seeking enterprises of the ancients, as a continuity can be traced, as will be seen hereafter, between those of the old and the present times. A survey of the past in such cases is useful in telling us what to eliminate and what to retain in the present.

It shall be our endeavour to shew generally that some of the ancient methods of obtaining gold have survived till the present time, and may be found now in many remote places. Certainly, in many places not remote, fanciful ideas still exist concerning how gold can be found, and the origin of these may be traced in some of the following notes.

There is something in the occurrence of gold in nature which makes it either very easy or very difficult to obtain, according to the way of dealing with it. When it is obtained it is easily marketed, and this, too often in the past, tempted the workmen or highwaymen to annex it between the mine and its owners. With other metals, such as copper and iron, the circumstances are different. These generally occur in nature as sulphides or oxides, and always require long processes to make them marketable, and their weight, even when converted into bars, makes it difficult for the thief to carry them away.

The most ancient gold-seekers chiefly looked for nuggets and dust of gold, but they also mined quartz veins containing gold to a limited depth.

ANCIENT GOLD FIELDS.

Among the more important ancient gold workings were the following :—

Phœnicia.—This was a little country, a strip containing about 4,000 square miles, in the north-east portion of the Levant. Its capital was Tyre, which was "A merchant of the people for many Isles."—Ezekiel xxvii. 3. It produced, at home, dyes and cloth, and traded with its manufactures in ships to distant parts where mines were opened up. In the language of to-day the Phœnicians were in the "Soft goods trade"—linen, woollen, and silk ; they were also "timber merchants," and probably "grain merchants," as well as ship-owners, miners, metallurgists, and art metal-workers like the Birmingham braziers. (See Note 1.) One of their earliest colonies was the island of Cyprus, where they extracted copper, which metal was called "Cuprum" after the island. They established many colonies, but they appear to have worked for gold particularly in what is now known as Andalusia, in Spain, and in that part of Africa now known as Rhodesia.

An account of an ancient Phœnician mine is given in the Book of Job, chap. xxviii. verses 1-11, which is only intelligible, however, to the English reader in the revised version.

In North Africa, Carthage was founded by discontented Phœnicians, who in their turn continued the enterprising habits of the parent state, and appear to have sought for gold in the west coast of Africa, where now a great modern gold field is worked.

Colchis.—On the Asiatic side of the Caucasus. Here probably Jason came to find the "Golden Fleece." The mythical tale of Jason and the Argonauts may have a germ of truth in its origin if we consider Jason as merely a high-spirited adventurer anxious to find the source of gold beyond the seas. He sought forty-nine comrades to navigate his ship to the land of the "Golden Fleece," where they caught the river-gold on fleeces of sheep. This practice is said to exist still among the natives in South America. It was quite common till recently to use woollen blankets for the same purpose, the gold which had escaped amalgamation being entangled and held up in the woollen texture of the material.

Urals.—Ancient workings which must date back before the Tartar Conquest have been found along the borders of the Ural Mountains. (See Note 2.)

India.—Gold is widely distributed in India, and was worked in remote antiquity; but only in a few localities does it occur in sufficient quantity to make its systematic working at the present day remunerative. Ancient writers like Herodotus, Strabo, and Pliny make mention of the gold of India, and tell strange stories as to its being dug up in the form of dust by ants of gigantic size. (See Note 3.) Vast stores of gold were formerly possessed by the native princes in parts of Southern India, enabling them to construct works costing millions of money. Much of the treasure of the Rajahs fell into the hands of the Moslem invaders in the fourteenth century, and was carried to Delhi. Ancient workings on an extensive scale have been found in Madras, and probably much of the gold was formerly ob-

tained from the Wynaad and the Colar district of Mysore, where important mines are at present worked. It appears that the ancient miners followed very accurately the course of the reefs. Gold washing is still carried on in many parts of India by natives who work according to ancient methods which have been preserved traditionally.

China, Japan.—There are also ancient mines in these countries. Japanese historians refer the discovery of gold in their country to the year 749 of our era. During the sixteenth and seventeenth centuries great quantities of gold were obtained by the Portuguese and the Dutch. The gold of Japan occurs in quartz veins and in alluvial gravels, but in neither case are the deposits rich. Most of the gold now obtained is from mixed ores containing silver and other metals.

Asia-Minor, Lydia.—The sands of the river Pactolus yielded abundant gold, and from that source was derived the wealth of Crœsus.

Lydian stone is a very hard compact siliceous rock, often containing fractures filled in by fine layers of quartz. It consists of an intimate mixture of silica, alumina, carbonaceous material, and oxide of iron, and occurs in the Silurian and later Palæozoic formations. It was first brought from Lydia, and is used as a touch-stone for trying the purity of gold.

Africa-Ophir-Fur-Afur.—Modern investigations have proved that the Phœnicians worked for gold in what is now known as Rhodesia on a very extensive scale; in fact, of the two hundred or more gold mining companies now carrying on operations there, in this twentieth century, nearly every one is working on a lode which was anciently worked by the Phœnicians, while in their vicinity some 500 ruined buildings attest the presence, for long periods of time, of this enterprising people.

Many authorities are now convinced that these were the mines from which Solomon obtained his riches, and that Africa is the land of Ophir or Fur mentioned in Holy Writ.

The present age is much indebted to the inhabitants of Tyre and Sidon for opening up these (now Rhodesian) mines. They, moreover, only worked them down to a depth of about 100 feet. Deep sinking is entirely a modern accomplishment, rendered possible by the introduction of Watt's Steam Engine late in the eighteenth century.

Not only can their cities and temples be seen, but their forts in strategic positions, protecting the roads leading to the sea at Sofala, where the gold of Ophir was shipped to Tyre and Sidon. We also find in the ruins the old gold-smelting furnaces, as well as crucibles and blow-pipes with splashes of gold on the nozzles. (See Note 4.)

Moulds used for casting the ingots have been found of the same shape as those used by the Phœnicians in smelting tin in Cornwall. The late Mr. Bent's Book contains an illustration of the form of Ingot (Astragulus or bone shaped). By the courtesy of Mrs. Bent and the publishers, Messrs. Longmans, the figure is reproduced below. The moulds themselves may be seen in the Museum at Capetown. (See Note 5).

It is obvious that in this ancient Ophir or Fur, called by the Moors Afur, a vast organization was in existence for gold extraction, the methods of which were very different from those of the present times.

Mr. G. R. Carey has described the occurrence of these ancient workings, and their significance to the modern prospector. He has also described the methods of mining and blasting the rock with fire and water, afterwards breaking it down with hammers, and the crushing of the ore on flat stones, which eventually became hollowed. (See Note 6.)

Egypt.—Similar claims to being the ancient Ophir have been put forward on behalf of the re-discovered mines in the district lying between the Nile Valley and the Red Sea. About 25 years ago a papyrus was discovered giving a map of the mines in the Akita district. In the reign of Seti I. of the XIX dynasty, wells were opened along the route so that these mines might be

reopened, and even at that time they were spoken of as of great antiquity. Diodorus refers to the mines of Nubia and Ethiopia, and says they were worked by captives of war and criminals. It is known from documentary evidence that the quantity of gold obtained in ancient times from the Eastern desert must have been enormous. Professor Sayce has said that for several centuries "Egypt was the California of the ancient civilized world of the East." Quite recently Mr. C. J. Alford has visited many of the old mining sites, where he found remains of the miners' huts, in some cases in irregular groups forming villages or small towns. Relics of the old mining appliances occur in the form of old quartz mills, each consisting of an upper and a lower grindstone, and also of elliptical rubbing stones on which it would seem that the quartz was pulverized by attrition with a stone rolling-pin. Workings have recently been resumed on some of these ancient sites. (See Note 7.)

Italy.—Mr. Jervis says that the traces of alluvial gold washings seen in the province of Alexandria may, in all probability, be ascribed to the times of the Romans. They are, however, known to have found that the Salassi worked iron mines, and washed the alluvial gold of several Alpine torrents on the left of the Po. in the present province of Turin.

With his usual vague geographical information, Pliny speaks of the gold extracted to the north of Vercelli, and refers to the law limiting the number of persons to be employed in gold-seeking at 5,000. Local writers have striven to prove that Pliny alluded to the auriferous gravels of the Bessa region near Biella, but it would appear far more reasonable to conceive that he had been imperfectly informed of gold mining near the foot of Monte Rosa, above the present village of Alagna Valsesia, which is situated precisely at the head of the Val Sesia, near the source of the river Sesia, which

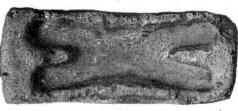

BONE SHAPED INGOT IN GOLD FROM SET LING'S KING OF MASHONAL AND. (See p. . .)

flows close by Vercelli. Nor could the Romans have failed to learn of the gold towards the eastern slopes of Monte Rosa, in the Val Anzasca.

Auriferous gold lodes are very numerous in the Piedmontese Alps between Mont Blanc and the Val Antigorio, east of the Simplon pass, and the number of the gold mines is considerable; but since many of them lie idle for years, the number of those in working condition fluctuates very much, from 15 to 25. (See Note 8.)

Andalusia in Spain.—The gold was washed down from the mountains in the river Guadalquiver, and the Toro del Oro at Seville is said to have been built either by the Phœnicians or their successors, the Romans, as a magazine for the precious metal.

From the mines around the port of Huelva they extracted a complex metal rich in gold by a smelting process, the slags of which, remaining to-day in vast quantities, attest their vigorous operations.

Spain.—Jervis in his Dell 'Oro in Natura says (see Note 9), "We have confidence in affirming that gold was obtained in ancient times by the Phœnicians and the aborigines of Andalusia, from the upper part of the pyrites lodes at Huelva, towards the outcrop, and from the auriferous alluvium derived from thence: but all this has been worked out centuries ago. There are sufficient indications of ancient mining operations made in the upper parts of the lodes. The Tyrenian colonists compelled the natives to work for them, and for the same purpose brought over slaves bought at Carthage. Both silver and a small quantity of gold are mentioned as products of the mines near Gadir."

"Historians relate that Hannibal obtained from the province of New Carthage, in Spain, the gold and silver necessary for him to prosecute the war against Rome."

Great Britain.—Judging from the gold ornaments which are occasionally found in burial mounds, it is believed that gold must have been obtained in this country as far back as prehistoric times. In a grave beneath a cairn near the Cheeswring in Cornwall, there was found, in 1818, a gold cup weighing 2 ozs. 10 dwts. This may, of course, have been imported; but grains or "prills" of gold were commonly found by the old tin-streamers, who worked the sands of the Cornish rivers, and preserved the precious metal in quills.

The Welsh triads make frequent mention of golden objects like torques and shields, cups, cars, and corslets, among the possessions of the old chieftains of the country. Relics of Roman workings for gold have been found at Gogofau, near Llandovery, in Caermarthenshire. In modern times gold was discovered in Merionethshire by Mr. Arthur Dean, in the year 1843. Since then the metal has been found widely distributed through the quartz veins of the neighbourhood of Dolgelly and Barmouth, and is at present the object of systematic exploration.

It is known that in *Scotland* much gold was formerly obtained from alluvial deposits in the burns of Crawfurd Moor, including Leadhills in Lanarkshire, and Wanlockhead in Dumfriesshire. The celebrated "bonnet pieces" of James IV. and V. were coined from the gold of this district. It is recorded that between 1538 and 1542 the workings, which were in charge of a goldsmith named John Mossman, yielded gold in such quantity that 113 ounces were used in making crowns for James V. and his queen, and for other royal ornaments. Late in the sixteenth century, Sir Bevis Bulmer, who worked the mines, presented to Queen Elizabeth a porringer made of the gold of Scotland. Gold may still be obtained in small quantity from the district of Crawfurd Moor; and the metal in recent years has been found in other parts of Scotland, especially in Sutherlandshire. (See Note 10.)

Ireland.—Alluvial gold has been obtained from the sands of many rivers in Ireland, principally from the streams on the northern slopes of Croghan Kinshela, a mountain in County Wicklow. About the year 1795 great excitement arose in consequence of rich discoveries at this locality, and hundreds of peasants flocked to the workings. It is said that the largest nugget obtained at this time weighed more than 20 ozs. The Government soon took over the operations, but in 1798 they were abandoned in consequence of the unsettled state of the country. Workings were resumed, however, in 1800; and from time to time since then have been spasmodically undertaken, but not with pronounced success. (See Note 11.)

Mexico, 1521.—When Cortez arrived in the West Indian Isles he was assured of a liberal grant of land to settle on. "But I came to get gold" replied Cortez, "not to till the soil like a peasant."

He organized an expedition to Mexico, and the story is fully unfolded in Prescott's history of the Conquest of Mexico, the early books of which represent Cortez being dazzled with the gifts of the king Montezuma—these were vases and plates of gold, a wicker basket filled with ornaments of wrought gold, shields, helmets, cuirasses embossed with plates and ornaments of pure gold, collars and bracelets of gold, a circular plate of gold as large as a carriage wheel weighing 3800 ounces, engraved in a most elaborate way, and valued in the currency of those days at £52,000 stg., as the beauty of the workmanship exceeded the value of the gold, a golden eagle with outspread wings and boots or sandals trimmed with gold-embossed gold plate. Cortez received 3000 ounces of gold on one occasion in a present, on another occasion he got a Spanish helmet filled to the brim with gold dust. Gold was the most frequent form of gift from the Indians to the Spaniards, as the Indians had learned to know their keen appetite for the metal. Such treatment only inspired the Spaniards more to possess the land.

Cortez' letter to Charles V. asserted that "the land teemed with gold as abundantly as that whence Solomon drew the same precious metal for his temple."

The gold came from the surface or was gleaned from river beds, and cast into bars or kept in the form of dust.

The gold dust was put into quills, and so used for what little currency they required.

When the conflict came between Spaniard and Mexican the fight was between the copper or bronze lances of the Indians and the Toledo steel of the Spaniards. (See Note 12.)

The treasure obtained was drawn from the accumulation of gold during a great many ages. The principal use the Spaniards noted

Mexicans put the gold to, as referred to above, was to display it on their persons and their buildings, and this conveyed the idea to the Spaniards that there were vast treasures, or at least mines of great quantities of gold somewhere.

They thought the barbaric display of gold on their persons and buildings only samples, and consequently that there was a great deal more gold easily obtainable than there really was.

Peru, 1532.—The invasion of Peru followed that of Mexico, the motive—gold—being the same. When Pizarro conquered Peru he and his followers were amazed at the large quantities of gold which the Incas possessed, not as coin, but worked into ornaments and even into utensils. This gold they obtained chiefly from the rivers. Like other ancient people, they could not mine to any depth, but were generally satisfied with what they got by merely scratching the surface. Their method of extraction was equally crude, the rude furnaces being built on exposed spots to catch the wind. When Pizarro captured their king it was arranged by his subjects to ransom him. The ransom of the Inca king Atahuallpa is valued by Prescott at nearly three and a half million pounds sterling. This was originally in the form of goblets, ewers, salvers, vases of every size and shape, ornaments and utensils for the temples and royal palaces, tiles and plates for the decoration of public edifices, curious imitations of different plants and animals, but Pizarro had them melted down to ingots of a uniform size. (See Note 13.)

The Spaniards made the same mistake here as in Mexico; they saw on the persons and on the houses of the Peruvians a great deal of gold, and did not know that it was the hoarded accumulation of long periods of time, and they consequently were disappointed that they could not find in the country an amount equal to the collection of the Incas. On page 205 will be seen the small position occupied at the present day by Peru as a producer of gold.

Eldorado. In Spanish "the Golden." This is a mythical place in the northern part of South America, probably including Venezuela and the Guianas. The Spaniards, being dazzled by the wealth of earlier conquests, indulged in much brilliant imagination. Expedition after expedition failed to find the city called Manoa, said to be in alliance with the Incas of Peru, which lavished the precious metals on its roofs and walls.

Even at the beginning of the 17th century this phantom exerted a master influence on Sir Walter Raleigh, and led up to the disastrous expedition to British Guiana for which eventually he was beheaded in 1618 on the charge of shedding Spanish blood. (See Note 14.)

Before leaving this part of the subject which is herein termed Ancient, the following chronology may prove interesting. By referring to the table of the World's production of Gold on pages 203 and 205 it will be readily seen that the division is quite naturally drawn between the old and the new by the statistical position of the production of gold which started upon the discovery of gold in California and Australia.

1537. United States of Colombia. New Granada—Gold Mining commenced by Spaniards.

1577. Brazil—the placers discovered but not worked actively till 1674. Product became important about 1695.

1695. Brazil—the rich placers of Minas Geraes began to produce largely.

1737. Russia—Voitsk.

1745. Russia—Ural and Siberia.

1774. Russia Ural—the first placers discovered, Quartz lodes having been opened 30 years previously.

1805. Bolivia—Ancosta.

1829. Georgia—United States of America. This was the first mining excitement in the U. S. A.

Modern Gold Fields.

The following list in chronological order (see Note 15) presents the principal modern gold fields the era of which may be safely reckoned, as stated above, from the discovery of alluvial gold in California. It will be observed that the discovery of alluvial gold has been usually the precursor of the later discovery of quartz veins.

1848. California—Alluvial at Coloma discovered by Marshall.

1849. Venezuela—Yuruari River.

1850. California—Quartz mining began.

1851. New South Wales—Count Strzelecki is said to have found gold in New South Wales in 1839, but in deference to the wishes of the Governor, Sir G. Phipps, the discovery was kept secret, the colony being then a penal one. In 1841, Rev. W. Clarke also found gold, and in 1847 he called the attention of the colonists to the auriferous character of the country. The value of the diggings was not realized, however, until Hargreaves made his discovery in 1851.

Victoria—Ballarat and Bendigo.

1852. South Australia.

Tasmania.

1857. New Zealand.

1858. Queensland—Canoona.

1859. British Columbia—Fraser River.

1861. Nova Scotia.

Oregon—Placers.

1862. Montana.

1864. Montana—Last Chance Gulch rich placers.

1866. Venezuela — Yuruari district, El Callao Mine.

1867. New Zealand — Thames goldfield north island.

1868. Western Australia—but no important diggings found till 1887.

1873. Transvaal—Pilgrim's Rest alluvial.

1876. Dakota—Black Hills began to attract attention.

Montana—Marysville Drumlummon Quartz Mine discovered.

1880. Southern India—Mysore Colar.

1883. Queensland—Rockhampton—Mount Morgan Gold Mine began to produce.

1884. Transvaal—De Kaap district discovered.

1885. Transvaal—Banket formation discovered on the Witwatersrand district. Active operations not commenced till 1887.

1888. Transvaal.—Pilgrim's Rest. Theta Reef discovered. The cutting of this reef demonstrated that there was a regular bedded formation carrying gold in some parts of the Oliphant limestone formation. This formation extends over a large portion of the Transvaal and other parts of South Africa.

1891. Rhodesia—Mashonaland begins to attract attention in modern times.

1897. Klondyke—Alluvial.

THE INCOMING OR DEVELOPEMENT OF THE SCIENTIFIC PERIOD IN GOLD MINING.

When the "alluvial" fields of California and Australia were first discovered, it was only the nuggety gold which was sought for amongst the river sands, and the value of the hard rocks was not realized.

If we refer to the annals of these goldfields, it will be found what a terribly wild speculation this gold-finding proved to be. Stories of the wonderful finds of those days linger in the memory of people still living. Wild, lawless, uncontrolled men flocked to those countries from every part of the world to make their fortunes in a day; and in extravagance and debauchery the majority spent it as fast as they had gained it.

It was slow work, after the subsidence of that gold fever, for a legitimate gold industry to establish itself; yet such an industry did spring up in California and Australia. Its development, however, was slow, and the early result of the mining and milling of gold-carrying quartz rock was not encouraging.

Too great haste has been often shown by the so-called "practical" man, whether capitalist or miner, to get at the gold, his only chance of profit. Such men always defeat the object they have in view; for it is only a proper understanding of the way in which gold is locked up within the gravel, or the sand and clay, the product of the stamps, that leads to a comprehension of the true method of obtaining gold cheaply, at a rate which will offer profit to capitalists. Briefly, it is the proper handling of these hard or intractable substances which wh

render it possible for any one to win the gold from their embraces. It is, therefore, necessary to understand in some degree the distribution of gold as seen in nature.

THE NEED OF SUITABLE ORGANIZATION.

The ancient and modern goldfields having now been passed rapidly under review, it may be asked can this business be removed more and more from the doubtful region of risk and speculation, and take its place as a recognised branch of scientific commerce?— The germ of an answer may be found in some of the following paragraphs.

Men entirely devoid of false ideas about every other business have entered the gold industry with sentimental tendencies towards the royal metal which lead them to spend more money in finding an ounce of gold than that ounce of gold is worth. There is, however, after all, nothing in the business which promises other than reasonable returns for intelligent industry and results won by the "Sweat of the face."

In demonstrating how the best results are to be achieved, it is necessary to clearly outline a convenient organization of the various departments of the work, technical and otherwise, which contribute to the successful mining and extraction of the gold from the stony matrices in which it exists in nature. It is by a clear conception on the part of the directors as to what they want from their officials, that the latter may know exactly what is expected of them, and by the keeping of a systematic record of work done in the several departments, that the great possibilities of loss which lurk in the business may be reduced to a minimum, and the best possible results be obtained. At the same time it is to be noted that mere book-keeping alone will not give this clear conception.

Mention is often made of the absurd hope which has been cherished through all ages in the minds of men that veins of gold and silver might one day be found as large and as rich as those of the inferior metals. Even, as we have mentioned, such a wise man as Sir Walter Raleigh fell into a snare of this kind when he dreamt of his Eldorado; and from age to age, down even to the present time, enormous wealth has been squandered in this futile search after subterranean storehouses of gold. Nature herself, it must be said, somewhat fosters this delusion, by scattering nuggety gold here and there on the surface, in such profusion, as to suggest a great underground store of the metal imprisoned somewhere in the hills.

It is thus that ignorant and avaricious people have always been infatuated with gold mining, and in many cases they have gone to work without counting the cost, either to themselves or to others. So largely has this been the case, that those great authorities on economics, who have taken the trouble to enquire into the facts, have often made the statement that gold costs more to produce than it is worth. This arises from gold mining having been hitherto so much a speculative employment. Many of those, however, who embarked on it in the past lost their money through ignorance as much as through speculation, and from the effects of a combination of these two, even bounteous nature cannot always avert disaster, with the result that the average earnings of the business have been relatively low.

The losses until quite recently have often been larger than the gains, and gold-mining enterprises have but too frequently brought bankruptcy to many of those engaged in them. Fortunately, however, recent years have seen a marked improvement in the business.

During the course of last century, and until lately, while other industries have been developed by science and capital, that of getting gold, the metal which from time immemorial has been used as a token or representative of the value of the wealth of the world, has been largely left in the hands of those possessed of but few of the special qualifications now required of those who engage in the business.

As a rule, pseudo-geologists, or prospectors but partially trained, were employed by men unable to judge of their qualifications, to survey and report on their properties. On the mine unqualified persons, in many instances, were employed to superintend the industrial part of the work, that

is, the mining, milling, and saving of the gold.

This incapable handling of the gold industry was so patent to the commercial world, that until lately prudent capitalists avoided gold-mining altogether as an investment.

Much has been done during the last 20 years in organizing the administration of gold mines, but even yet, owing to confusion arising in the minds of unskilled persons, who somehow or other have been introduced into the business, the work of the different departments has often become hopelessly mixed. By such persons, for instance, the manager is expected to be at the same time the geologist, the miner, the mechanic, the metallurgical chemist, and the business administrator, which inevitably leads to failure, just as a steamship would soon be on the rocks if the captain were expected to act as sailing master, engineer, steward, and purser.

Of course it must be borne in mind that in a small mine the management of different departments must sometimes be combined, when a man's time might not otherwise be fully occupied, just as on a coaster there is not the same sub-division of duties as on an ocean liner, but care in such cases must be taken to combine duties that are to a certain extent cognate. It is interesting here to note that the word "captain" has long been in use for the manager of a mine as well as of a ship, and also that the word "log-book" is commonly in use in mining business.

In the middle of last century, when the steamship business was in its infancy, many were the misunderstandings and discussions which arose over the relative positions and duties of the sailing masters and the marine engineers, till these were eventually organized on a definite footing. The writer had some opportunity of observing the process going on, and when he became interested in mining it occurred to him that in a similar way some definite rules of organization should be laid down as a basis for establishing the same conditions in mining administrations. In order to arrange each of the offices in its proper place he endeavoured to ascertain from the best practice the several necessary divisions which require each a different kind or type of man to carry on the work.

The following seem to embrace all the departments of a fully organized mine :—

A AND B—GEOLOGICAL MINE SURVEYING.
C—MINING ENGINEERING.
D—MECHANICAL AND ELECTRICAL ENGINEERING.
E—CHEMICAL ENGINEERING.

GENERAL MANAGEMENT.

1 TO 8—COMMERCIAL SUPERINTENDENCE OR MINES SECRETARIAL DEPARTMENT.
9—ASSAYING.

The indicating letters and numbers represent the various forms outlined in the body of this work.

The first five of these are purely technical.

The General Manager has control of all the technical as well as the commercial departments. It is the wise combination of qualities for these two departments which go far to contribute towards the success of gold-mining business.

The Commercial Superintendent or Mines Secretary is a purely commercial officer, but he should have some idea of the proportion and different kinds of work done by the technical departments, in compiling the forms of accounts and statistics, and the following notes of the scope of these technical departments may be of service to him as well as to all other commercial men who may be, or wish to be, concerned in gold mining.

The assaying is shewn upon the commercial side, although it is a technical department ; but it is placed here, as this work should be done as a check upon the working of the practical side of the operations.

Each of these divisions is dealt with in the following paragraphs, and it will be seen from the initial letters that they correspond with the technical departments set out on pages 42 to 88, while the initial numbers correspond with the various commercial books set out on pages 90 to 172.

A and B—GEOLOGICAL MINE SURVEYING—FORMERLY CALLED PROSPECTING.

Geology and kindred sciences, as well as experience, have taught us to avoid many errors, and the material laws of nature, as revealed by science, now help us, and as they themselves become better known, will tell us more of what we may, and what we may not expect, to find.

A general knowledge of the geology of gold-bearing veins and strata is necessary to successful gold-mine surveying, otherwise the existence of the lode or ore-body will remain much longer in doubt than is necessary. Proper geological surveys must take the place of the old prospector's empirical work, in order to prepare the field for the tools of the workers of the mines, who cannot otherwise proceed intelligently with their operations.

The face of nature, much of which, in olden times, appeared mystical and incomprehensible, is now unveiled, and may be seen and known by those who seek her earnestly. The result is, that we look for no subterranean treasure-house of gold, but only for the "mineralised" or metal-bearing beds of rock, which must be worked industrially before they yield up their treasures.

Gold is found in very small quantities disseminated through the mass of granitic mountains ; but to grind up such mountains for their gold would, of course, be a costly and unremunerative operation. It is locally distributed in many alluvial deposits, and it is also found in sea water, in the proportion of about one grain to the ton.

Geologists have taught us that during the long course of ages the mountains have been disintegrated and worn down by rain, snow, frost, and by river and sea action ; and the quartz, felspar, and other minerals, which are their principal constituents, have been laid down on sea shores and bottoms as gravel, sand, and clay. Piled up in massive beds, they formed in time conglomerates, sandstones, and mudstones, and were afterwards elevated by earth-movements, and built up into solid lands and mountains. It is in this way, the great geological writers point out, how the gold and other mineral contents of the rocks have ever been travelling along with the pebbles, sands, and clays, for countless ages of time ; and, shifting from mountain to plain, and from plain to sea, they have been crushed, crumpled, and metamorphosed by pressure, heat, and chemical changes, resulting from repeated earth-movements; and thus the gold, having been segregated and concentrated, is found in quartz and other veins in these newer formations.

Earth - movements, which have been going on from the earliest to the latest geological times, have caused great fissures in the earth's crust. Many of these fissures descend to unfathomed depths, and have formed vents or chimneys for the escape of gases and steam, carrying metals, including gold. These vapours were condensed, and the solutions were deposited in these fissures and cracks ; and the solid contents of these now form the lode-matter of mineral veins, so often pyritous and containing gold. In a group of such veins it often happens, however, that only a few are auriferous. Many cracks and fissures may also have been filled up by infiltrations, by the rain-water of the surface, carrying vein-matter containing gold denuded from the mountain sides, and by circulating waters dissolving mineral matter from the surrounding rocks.

Pyritous ores lying in any position near the earth's surface, and above the level of the water saturating the rocks, absorb oxygen to combine with their sulphur and iron, and thus become more or less iron oxides and sulphate of iron. Pyritous ores in deeper places below the water-level retain their sulphur, and from such ores it is always more difficult to extract the gold. The former are generally classed as free-milling ores, the latter as refractory.

The deposition of gold with conglomerates, sandstones, and schists, which have arisen from the destruction of older rocks, represents one class of auriferous deposits.

Still newer and more recent deposits with gold are represented by gravel, sand, and clay, worked out of old rocks, and laid in river terraces and bottoms of valleys. In California and Australia the river beds in many cases have been filled up with lava flows, forming a crust over the gravel, and and so the auriferous deposits have been protected from subsequent denudation in what are called "deep leads." It appears that the largest amount of gold obtained by the world's working has been derived from sedimentary rocks, comprising both alluvia and old strata.

We now know from geological observations that during the course of the alternating process by which continents are destroyed and then re-built, only some of the gold, and that a very small part, is to be found on the surface of the earth as nuggets, though a larger part may be found as gold dust. As the countries of the world were peopled, this gold was rapidly picked up by the first settlers, the gold of the ancients coming mainly from this source.

To follow these natural interchanges and results intelligently aids us to find out the general direction of the ore bodies as they lie in the earth's structure.

Further detail on the question of the origin of the geological conditions of gold-bearing deposits need not here be given. Enough has been said to show that the study of the nature of the enclosing matter, of the quartz and felspar rocks, or of the derivative gravel, sand, and clay, is an essential part of knowledge required by those engaged in the gold industry. For a list of useful books on this subject by Phillips and Louis, Kemp and others, see Notes 16 and 20.

The geologist and mineralogist not only prepare the way for the miner, but also for the gold-extractor, because a preliminary knowledge of the chemical and physical conditions of the ore body enables the owners of mines to erect extraction works suitable for the saving of the gold found under the peculiar circumstances of each case.

The ore in sight and the life of a mine should be carefully estimated, and Mr. Kendall's recommendations, as set out on page 38, should be studied. The costs of preliminary and concurrent surveys by competent geologists should always be provided for in any gold-mining scheme. The expense of such surveys will be infinitesimal compared with the money thrown away in times past on abortive Eldorado-like schemes.

C.—Mining.

Following the mining geologist comes the mining engineer, who opens up the lode or deposit in such a manner that it may be worked in the most economical and profitable way. This having been done, and sufficient ore body having been developed, it remains for the mechanical engineer to erect mills for crushing the lode stuff, and for the amalgamator or chemist to actually extract the gold from the ore.

In rocks containing gold, the precious metal is usually disseminated through the whole mass; and an idea of the searching character of the work necessary to get one ounce of gold from the ton of ore may be formed by remembering that in an avoirdupois ton of rock-matter there are 32,666 troy ounces which have to be ground up and sorted out or otherwise dealt with, to get from them that one ounce troy of gold. The proportion of gold contained in a ton of such matter is thus ·00306 or ₃₂₆₆₆ of the whole. It must easily be seen what delicate and thorough work is required to save such relatively small quantities of gold.

To illustrate this in a graphic manner the author had two cubes constructed, one to represent the size of a ton block of ordinary quartz, the other to represent the size of one ounce of gold, and exhibited these at the Philosophical Society of Glasgow, when a paper on this subject was read to that Society on 7th November, 1894. On later occasions the blocks were shown at a meeting of the Geologists' Association, London, on 7th June, 1895; in 1899, at the Greater Britain Exhibition (Rhodesian Court) at Earl's Court, London; in March and April, 1902, at the Colonial Exhibition (Rhodesian Court), at Royal Exchange, London; and in May, 1902, at the Exhibition (Rhodesian Court), held at Imperial Institute, London.

For comparison, let it be noted that in the copper industry usually about 150 lbs. of copper are recovered from 2,240 lbs. of ore, and that in the iron industry about 1,120 lbs. of iron are recovered from 2,240 lbs. of ore, so that it is at once seen how relatively small in the case of gold ores is the amount of metal extracted to the amount of ore handled.

The mining operations should be under the control of an educated and experienced mining engineer, who should have had experience in mining various ores in different parts of the world. It is a great disadvantage to employ a miner whose prejudices have been developed by long experience in one particular series of rocks or the physical structure of one region. Such a man, however capable otherwise, has no resources when he comes to deal with new geological conditions. Unfortunately, many good mines have been condemned by such men.

Having considered the distribution in nature of rock-matters carrying gold, the cost of bringing these auriferous ores "to grass," and their delivery to the mills for the extraction of the gold should now be investigated.

The various methods of gold-mining naturally depend on the formation of the gold-bearing rocks. In some mines the ore is won through vertical shafts by winding machinery, and in others by inclined shafts or horizontal tunnels, in which tramways are worked by endless ropes. When the ore bed lies near the surface, it is sometimes found convenient to strip off the superincumbent mass of earth, or "overburden," and work the ore-bed as an open quarry. The river banks or terraces containing auriferous gravel and sand are "hydrauliced"; that is to say, the banks are washed away by powerful jets of water, and the gold is saved by catching it in boxes containing mercury placed along the bottom of "flumes," and river beds are now often dredged for gold.

All these methods open vast fields for the exercise of mining-engineering skill and enterprise. The commercial success of the venture depends as much on the proper development of the mine as on the actual gold contents of the ore.

In America there are many colleges for the training of mining engineers. In Europe there are fewer of such institutions, but generally speaking, for work such as has just been described, a preference should be given to a graduate of one of these colleges, provided he has had sufficient practical experience in addition. One of the advantages of such college training is that the student is made familiar with the scientific principles on which the various operations at the Mine, and at the Reduction Works are founded, and he thus is better equipped if the occasion arises to take general management of the whole, than if he only knew the work of his own department.

D.—Mechanical—Crushing the Ore.

Having followed the ore "to grass," as the miners call the surface, and delivered it to the mills, the next work to be done is to crush it fine enough to liberate the particles of gold. This is done by passing it, first, through a stone-breaker, in which the larger pieces are reduced, and then by crushing further in a stamping battery or other pulveriser.

The battery, as well as the preparatory rock-breaker, should be under the care of a practical mechanical engineer. It is not necessary that he should have had formerly much experience in batteries; but it is necessary that he should know the wearing qualities of different metals used in the battery. The battery is usually a mechanical arrangement of heavy hammers, which fall from 80 to 100 times per minute, and the steel heads of which are subject to enormous tear and wear. The chief subject for the consideration of the mill superintendent is the life of the wearing parts of the mill.

The battery is flushed with water, and the finely-divided ore (or "pulp") is carried through the gratings at the stamps and on to copper plates covering a table, over which it flows in a broad, thin stream. The surface of these plates is coated with mercury, which forms an amalgam with most of the larger particles of free gold while passing over the plates. The amalgam is scraped from the plates at intervals, and heated in a retort so as to separate and recover the mercury and the gold. This operation is called the "clean up." Unfortunately, all the gold is not caught on the plates, but a large percentage is carried away in the tailings of sand or clay, or in the water; and at this point, again, a knowledge of the enclosing rock-structure, and of the chemical and physical condition of the material carrying the gold, is necessary for success in saving this metal.

If the "gangue," or stony matrix of the gold, is felspathic in character, the felspar is reduced to clay by the stamping; and the water flushing the mill first deposits the sand of the quartz in the water channel or "launder," at the end of the tables, carrying off the clayey or flocculent matter to a greater distance, while sometimes more elaborate methods have been adopted to separate the products. This separation of sand and clay increases the difficulty of the after treatment of the tailings. With the sandy tailings there is a chance of recovering some of the gold by working them over again; but with the clayey tailings or "slimes," as they are called, it is more difficult to deal, and indeed, until the last half-dozen years no attempt was made to deal with them at all. There is no greater "thief of gold" in the mill than the clay. Take a ton of clay from a brickmaker's clay puddle, such as can be seen any day, add to it half-an-ounce of gold dust or gold leaf, and imagine the difficulty of recovering the gold from such slime.

The water used for flushing the mill is also a robber of gold. When the stamps used in crushing the ore strike very small pieces of the contained gold, they convert these into gold leaf.

The Californian stamp-mill for crushing the ore is an improvement in details and adaptability on the old Cornish mill used in tin-stamping, which has been in vogue since the seventeenth century.

E.—Metallurgical and Chemical Processes.

The catching of the gold on copper tables has been and is even now under the care of an officer, usually called an amalgamator. A good amalgamator, diligent at his work, and strictly honest and sober, might, by means of a keen observation and the acquired experience of many years, be able to improve the savings up to 30 or 40 per cent. of the gold contained in the ore, and only with very exceptional ores did the recovery exceed this. This, however, could only be obtained by long and special experience, and as the result of his empirical method of saving the gold. Such a man is always difficult to obtain. He is more an artist than a workman, and represents the type of man employed in the process of refining copper in the Swansea furnaces, whose precise method science has hardly yet been able to define.

A similar type of person, in a different employment, was the old-fashioned dairymaid, now long retired to the moorland farm if not wholly extinct. She tested the progress of the operation of cheese-making by the taste. If her palate was true and clean, she made good cheese; if not, the cheese was spoiled. In this rustic industry, also, science has replaced the old by new and different processes. Nowadays the operation is regulated by readings of the thermometer.

All empirical methods of working any business must eventually give way to scientific systems. It is evident that until quite recently the gold industry has been left far behind in the march of improvement. The history of abortive processes of gold-saving is a veritable record of struggles in the Slough of Despond. If any one will refer to Alfred G. Lock's excellent book on "Gold" (see Note 17), he will find there a long catalogue of processes which, though suggestive, have not been found practical in their application. It is well, however, to keep them in memory, as there is always a tendency for a different set of persons to try the same experiments over again.

At this point it may be mentioned that mines are often situated where there may be sufficient water for washing the ore, but where there is not sufficient fall in the water-level to supply power to drive the mills, and where the other source of power, fuel, is scarce. Until recently such mines could not be worked at a profit unless the ore was exceptionally rich, but electrical science has made such strides within the last few years that power generated by a water-mill at a distance of many miles can now be transmitted by cables, and utilised at mines or mills with a comparatively small percentage of loss of efficiency in transmission. The result is that operations

formerly impracticable can now be carried on at a profit.

The origin of modern chemistry springs from the searchings of the alchemists, whose aim was principally to make gold out of some other metal. It is strange that, while the ancient chemist devoted so much attention to gold, the modern chemist, until recently, left it severely alone; and, even though scientific chemists have now become alive to the importance of their science in its application to gold-extraction processes, the commercial and so-called practical men in charge of mines, as a rule, until recently did not see its full importance. In some parts of the world even yet, it is the exception to employ chemists, with the result that the gold lost in the tailings is left untold and unestimated. Such was the old style. Under the new style, every metal-extracting works for gold or other metals has a good practical metallurgical chemist, accustomed to work processes on the commercial scale, and who makes himself acquainted with all the new processes, and improvements in old processes.

The limitation of amalgamation by mercury to free-milling ores has caused gold-miners, as afore-mentioned, to look out for other methods of extraction. Smelting could only be profitably resorted to when the ores were extremely rich, as it would require too much fuel to do the work for poor ores, or where the ore might form a suitable flux for copper ore in the same district as the gold values are taken up by the copper matte, and afterwards recovered by the electrolytic process of refining.

Many chemical processes have been suggested and patented, but practically only two such systems have been successfully worked—namely, the "Chlorination" process, and the "Cyanide" process. The ores and tailings that are not amenable to amalgamation may generally be classed as sulphides, or as containing sulphides, with which the gold is in so intimate connection that it is difficult to attack the gold without at the same time attacking the sulphides, and so using an excessive quantity of the chemicals.

It is now most scarce of concentrates to copper smelting works, where such exist within easy reach.

Warnford Lock, in his book "Practical Gold Mining," Chap. VI. (see Note 18), describes various appliances for assisting or forcing amalgamation, such as Berdan's and Wheeler's Pans and the Hydrogen Amalgamator, and in Chap. VII, he describes many methods which are tried for treating rebellious ores with more or less success, such as Plattner's, Mears, Newberry-Vautin's, Pollock's and other chlorination methods. All these, however, are practically now superseded by the Cyanide Process, except in a few special cases, such as at the Mount Morgan Mine, where chlorination is still practised.

Cyanide Process.—This is the most recent of all the chemical processes, having only come into practical use in 1891, and, considering the short time that it has been in vogue, it has had an extraordinary influence on the gold industry in South Africa and other places. The process is applicable to most of the refractory ores and tailings, and one of its main advantages, besides its economy, is its simplicity, except when copper, arsenic, or tellurium is present—in such cases special treatment is required.

The ore, after having passed through the stamp battery and over the amalgamating tables, or in some cases after having been ground to a given fineness, wet or dry, without amalgamation, is put into large vats, of a capacity, in some cases, of 200 and 300 tons, and in these it is treated with a weak solution of cyanide of potassium. This dissolves the gold. The auriferous liquor is then run through boxes containing zinc in a fine state of division; and the gold is precipitated on the zinc, from which it is washed off at intervals. The mother liquor is pumped back to the supply tank, brought up to its original strength, and used over again. This process is known as the "MacArthur-Forrest."

It was long known that the cyanides had an affinity for metallic gold; but, as they had also an affinity for the baser metals, the extraction of gold from ores by this means was not considered feasible. Messrs. MacArthur & Forrest, however, discovered the interesting fact that "cyanide" in weak solutions had a strong selective affinity for gold, and that, by utilising this the economical recovery of gold from ores might be accomplished. The zinc used as the precipitant is in the form of filaments or fine shavings, prepared from the metal in a lathe, and pressed together to form a spongy mass, with a maximum of bright surface for a given weight. Modifications of the process have been in some cases adopted, such as the addition of bromo-cyanide to the solution, or the substitution of electric deposition for the zinc depositing boxes.

No attempt has been made in the foregoing description to enter into detail, but simply to give a general outline of the process.

In the earlier years of the process it was found that the presence of the clayey slimes among the sandy tailings interfered with the percolation of the dissolving liquor through the sands, and with the subsequent draining of the vats, and the slimes were therefore carefully separated from the sands, and at first were run to waste. Within the last few years, however, the slimes have also come to be successfully treated, especially on the Rand, where, after agitation with the cyanide liquor, the liquor and spent slimes are separated by decantation; and in Western Australia, where, as a rule, the agitation is followed by filter-press treatment for the purpose of facilitating the separation.

In "Cyanide Practice," by Alfred James (see Note 19), he says, "Possibly the most remarkable tribute to the efficiency of the Cyanide Process is the practical relegation to the background of the numerous processes which formerly so persistently reappeared under different names, and in the hands of different inventors, claiming highest possible extraction at a minimum of cost."

As an epoch-making date we note that the McArthur Forrest Patent was applied for in Oct., 1887.

GENERAL MANAGER.

Over all the departments there should be placed a General Manager, and much depends on the choice of a suitable man for this post.

He should have some knowledge of the work of all the technical departments, and be an expert or master in at least one of them.

Which of the many professions or trades which go to equip a mine staff he should be master of is not a difficult matter to decide.

It is found in general experience that the mining engineer generally makes the best manager, though there are certainly many instances where men with other training have well filled the post. It is essential that he be a good administrator in addition to his technical qualifications, so as to give scope to, and to utilize to the best advantage, the skill and intelligence of the various chiefs of departments, as well as to control their work.

In many countries the law demands that the mining operations be under the superintendence of a certificated manager, who has been properly trained, and has by examination shown his knowledge of the work and of the precautions required to enable it to be carried on with safety. Apart from other reasons, it is advisable that the man who is held responsible by the Government should be the man to control the whole operations at the mine.

While it is unreasonable to expect that he should be a good metallurgist and an experienced accountant at the same time as a highly trained mining expert, still a man who wishes to qualify for such an important post should at least know the rudiments of the different departments over which he is to exercise general control, so that he may be able to understand the principles involved, and convey intelligently to the heads of departments instruction which may be transmitted from head quarters.

1 TO 8. COMMERCIAL SUPERINTENDENT.

The Commercial Superintendent, or as he is sometimes called, the Mine Secretary, ought to be the Manager's first lieutenant. There is apt sometimes to be suspicion of this officer on the part of old fashioned managers, but his function is really to assist the Manager, and relieve him of work of

purely commercial and statistical nature, which in a large mine would otherwise absorb so much of the General Manager's time.

The most important part of this officer's work is seeing to the expenditure of the cash and stores, and that the preparation of the general expenditure sheets, showing the costs, without which the best of managers will be working in the dark, is properly carried out. It is also his duty, in conjunction with the Manager, to forecast the requirements of the mine in cash and stores, and for a period some months ahead of the needs.

In the old days, when amalgamation was the only method of extracting the gold from the ore, it was bad enough when the crude method of accounts did no more than enable one to tell at the end of the year whether there was a profit or a loss on the operation as the whole; but now when there are many delicate processes going on simultaneously, it is misleading to lump all costs together, as too many mining companies in some parts of the world still do, as one may have amalgamating, cyaniding of sands, cyaniding of slimes, and treatment of concentrates going on together, and if there be no means of ascertaining the costs for each department or process, a profit made in one department may be thrown away in part or wholly in other departments.

A proper system of ascertaining the costs would prevent such a practice as that adopted by a well known mine, which in a recent annual report explained that the profits in the half-year under review were higher than in the previous year, because the large stock of cyanide laid in and paid for during the previous six months was not yet all used up.

A man fit to be a Commercial Superintendent should previously have had experience in some of the subordinate positions set out in the Organization Book, either as wages clerk, stores clerk, or accountant, and he ought to have made himself acquainted to a considerable degree with the technicalities of the business.

To leave the Accounts to book-keepers

trained, or to managers who concern themselves little about the Accounts, generally leads to an unsystematized set of Accounts. The book-keeper's figures may be right so far as they go, but they do not go far enough; while managers may neglect the cash part of the Accounts as inconvenient, and spend money in useless work—stating the Accounts of their department rather as they would like the facts to appear, than as they really are, and so deceive both themselves and their Directors.

The system of Accounts here presented largely prevents anything of the kind, and also unites the final results of the work done from the ore to the ingot, with the cash paid for it, in one series of easily-checked returns.

Local officials should be obliged to render such a full and correct statement of their doings as will make it possible for Directors and Auditors at the Head Office at once to grasp the true state of affairs. This system is intended to throw a strong light upon the entire conduct of the business, and to enable a Director or Auditor to put his finger upon the very pulse of the whole concern.

If the forms are carefully filled up, they will soon show where any leakage is occurring, either in the outgoing of cash or stores, or the incoming of gold, and in that way provide a valuable check on what is going on.

When introduced at the outset in the case of new Companies, this system may prevent leaks occurring at all; and in the case of going-concerns, it may demonstrate the result of good management, and the evidence would certainly be of a more impartial character than where the system is devised by the manager himself.

Economic Importance of Systematic Accounts. — The judicious regulation of Mining affairs, by keeping proper Departmental Accounts, shewing either the efficiency or otherwise of the different methods and processes used, has become, of late years, most essential. There has been an influx into the Mining business both of capitalists and employees, who, until recently, were wholly unacquainted with Mining affairs; and it is therefore not to be wondered at that many book-keeping experiments have

been made, the effects of which are often misleading to the Directors of Companies. In view, therefore, of the importance of the subject and the amount of capital invested in foreign mines, it seems not out of place to offer a more uniform and transparent system of Mining Accounts than has hitherto been in use.

British mine owners should be able to regulate the expenditure at their mines abroad; but to do this, it is necessary that the records of work done and evidence as to the purposes for which the money has been spent, be of a satisfactory character.

Uniformity. — At present there is a great absence of uniformity in Mines Accounts; the returns sent home by the various managers and book-keepers being generally drawn up to suit themselves; and as mines are more likely to be controlled in groups in the near future, the first essential to proper control will be uniformity. Such grouping together will rather lend itself to uniformity.

Comparison. — When uniformity of Accounts is established, comparison is made possible, and this is helpful in arriving at a sound judgment about such questions as whether the mine will eventually pay at all or not, or whether the recovery process is an effective one, or the management faulty. These questions as to treatment or management are rapidly becoming the most important connected with Mining business, in view of the low grade quality of ore which, when properly dealt with, can now be turned to good account.

It frequently happens that, while the mine may be good, the process of recovering the metal may be bad or badly worked, and such a mine may go on for years paying profits, no doubt, but not such profits as are due from it with better management. With a proper system of Accounts and departmental records, the fault in treatment or management will be disclosed.

Some managers have complained that the appointment of a Commercial Superintendent is the introduction of a system of espionage and a reflection on their integrity, and a direct intimation that they are suspected by their Directors. The very opposite should result from such appointments in the administration of the commercial affairs of a mine, as many complications that arise in mine accounts are straightened out under a good system of organization, and the working difficulties of the management are always made plain, if the accounts reflect the true state of affairs.

9. ASSAYING.

The Assay Department in small mines may be conjoined to the Cyanide Department; but when the magnitude of the operations justifies it, a separate department should be created.

The assayer should be a properly trained chemist. He is often a junior who may be qualifying to take the more responsible duty of Metallurgical Superintendent when an opportunity for advancement arises.

The assayer should report direct to the general manager, and his report should either supply an assay plan of the developments, or supply the data on which such a plan can be constructed. His report should also deal with the results of the samples taken at various stages of the process of gold recovery, and shall either set forth the total results so as to show the percentage of recovery, loss in process, and loss in residues, or supply the figures in a way which will quickly enable this to be done.

The Assay Department on the technical side supplies the check on the process operation, which the Commercial Department does in regard to costs. In fact, it enables a balance sheet of the contents of the ore to be constructed.

An account should be kept showing the assay value of the total fine gold (see page 179) contained in the ore before it is milled, and of the fine gold produced therefrom. The difference unaccounted for should show the gold unrecovered in working the process —that is to say, the gold left in the spent ore, usually called the tailings of sand and clay, after full treatment, and the gold lost in the process.

When the amalgam of gold and mercury is taken from the copper plates, it is brought to the assay office and retorted. The mercury is distilled off, and the gold is left

in the resulting bullion. This is cast into ingots of about 250 ounces weight, and sent, after being refined, to the Mint. So, also, the precipitated gold from the cyanide solution is rubbed off the zinc, fused, and cast into bullion, its ultimate destination being also the Mint. The bars are assayed before being sent to the Mint, and are reported as being so many parts fine, 1,000 parts representing absolutely pure gold. The bars from amalgamated gold usually run about 800 to 900 parts fine, according to the ore treated. The remaining parts of the 1,000 may consist of silver, copper, or a little iron. An appreciable quantity of silver in the bullion is paid for by the buyers. Nothing is usually allowed for the other metals. The bars from cyanide-extracted gold are usually low in value, running from about 400 to 600 parts fine gold in 1,000. The impurity is principally zinc or lead from the extractor boxes.

The gold carried in the bullion when sold in London is at a fixed value.

PROFITS AND COSTS.

It is impossible to lay down any hard and fast line as to what the costs in different departments should be, as the conditions of working vary so greatly in different countries, and even in the same country, according to the scale on which the operations are conducted.

The wide variation and the general reduction of costs are shown in the tables of the late Mr. Hamilton Smith, and of Mr. Hennen Jennings, of the results obtained at well known gold mines during the last twenty years. (See page 201.)

It will be seen from these figures that on the Rand ore yielding 10 dwts. per ton can be treated at a considerable profit.

The influence of large output in reducing costs is shown in the results obtained at the Alaska Treadwell Mine, where ore yielding 3 dwts. per ton is treated at a cost under 5 shillings per ton.

It is claimed that there are mines working at a profit in Victoria on ores yielding 3 to 4 dwts. per ton, but their accounts are not available for inspection.

Mr. Alfred James states that "It is now possible to make considerable profits from tailings, assaying only 1 dwt. per ton, and even ores may be mined, crushed, and cyanided, as in Borneo, for 5 shillings and 6 pence per ton. (See Note 19.)

CONCLUSION.

The certain market at a fixed rate for the product of gold-mining is an advantage which other metallurgical industries have not, and removes all fear of falling prices, which is the constant disappointment of all other industries.

When the fair offers of profit are considered which nature and science hold out to the industrious and intelligent gold-miner, the question may be put—Will there not some day be a deluge of gold? Such questions arose when the Australian and Californian gold-fields were producing the large quantities of nuggets, and the output of South Africa and Western Australia suggests the same question to-day. It is not, however, probable that gold will be greatly depreciated in value relatively to other commodities, as it is restricted in its native distribution; and, moreover, it is so uniformly distributed in such very small particles throughout the rocks that great industry and intelligence are required to gather it into a compact form.

The late Professor Stanley Jevons wrote a paper in 1859, entitled, "Remarks on the Australian Gold Fields," in which he foreshadows the time "when greater experience is attained in quartz-mining, now so new an employment; when improved machinery is brought into use for the rapid, complete, and cheap extraction of the gold from the quartz matrix; when capital is attracted in great sums to the pursuit; and when the search for new auriferous reefs, becoming more keen, is rewarded," as he says he believes it will be, "by abundant discoveries." He finally draws two conclusions:

I. "That no great and recurring discoveries of alluvial gold are to be expected, so that the yield of alluvial gold must notably, yet gradually, fall off."

II. "That the supply of gold from its quartz matrix is subject to entirely different laws; that we at present know no limit to the amount procurable with the aid of capital; and that that amount, whatever it may be, will probably remain constant for a long period of time."

Mr. Jevons' conclusions have been wonderfully accurate, as will be seen by the statistics of the world's production. (See pages 203 and 205.)

It will be observed that the gold product fell off slightly till quite lately, owing to the failure of supplies from alluvial deposits; and it is now increasing owing to permanent supplies from rock-crushing, as he predicted. If we could show the gold from alluvial washing and quartz-crushing separately, the alluvial quantity would be a decreasing one, and the quartz-crushing a rapidly increasing one.

NOTES AND REFERENCES.

William Jacobs.—An Historical Inquiry into the Production and Consumption of the precious Metals. 2 Vols. London: Murray, 1831.

This inquiry was suggested to Mr. Jacobs by Mr. Huskisson, of Liverpool, before the mid-century discoveries were made of Gold in California and Australia, and shows the awakening of interest early last century as to what should be the proper industrial position of gold mining.

The book is a comprehensive history of Ancient Gold Fields, Mining, and Metallurgy.

NOTE.
1. Rawlinson's Phœnicia. London: Unwin.
2. Gold Fields, Ancient and Modern. Westminster Review, 1883, pages 378-408.
3. V. Ball—A Manual of the Geology of India, Part III. Calcutta: 1881.
4. Hall & Neal's Ancient Ruins of Rhodesia. London: Methuen & Co., 1902.
5. Bent's Ruined Cities of Mashonaland. London: Longman, 1892.
6. Carey's Gold Mining in Matabeleland; a paper read before the Institution of Mining and Metallurgy, April, 1902.
7. Alford's Gold Mining in Egypt, read before the Institution of Mining and Metallurgy, October, 1901.
8. Chevalier Jervis' I Tesori Sotterranei dell' Italia. Turin: Loescher, 1889.
9. Chevalier Jervis' Dell' Oro in Natura. Turin: Roux & Favale, 1881.
10. Heddle's Mineralogy of Scotland. Edinburgh: Douglas, 1901.
11. G. A. Kinahan's Mode of Occurrence and Winning of Gold in Ireland, read before the Royal Dublin Society, March, 1882.

12. Prescott's History of the Conquest of Mexico, 3 vols. London: Bentley, 1847.

13. Prescott's History of the Conquest of Peru, 3 vols. London: Bentley, 1847.

14. Encyclopedia Britannica. Art., El Dorado.

15. The Mineral Industry. Vol. I., 1892. Supplies the principal dates of the chronology of discoveries of the different gold fields from 1442, page 225. Scientific Publishing Co., New York.

16. Phillips & Louis—A Treatise on Ore Deposits. London: Macmillan, 1896.

17. Alfred G. Lock—Gold. London: Spons.

18. Warnford Lock—Practical Gold Mining. London: Spons.

19. James—Cyanide Practice. London: Spons.

20. Kemp—The Ore Deposits of the United States and Canada. New York and London: The Scientific Publishing Co., 1900.

Louis—A Handbook of Gold Milling. The reader is recommended to peruse the definitions of the occurrence of Gold on pages 2 to 5. London: Macmillan, 1894.

Curle—Gold Mines of the World. London: Waterlow & Sons, 1902.

Brough—The Nature and Yield of Metalliferous Deposits. Cantor Lectures, before the Society of Arts, July 27th, 1900, page 690.

Mr. Brough says—"Gold has been worked in rocks of eruptive origin. It has been found in recent lava, and its presence has been detected in sea water. It is therefore quite unsafe to prophesy, as has so often been done in the past, that any particular geological formation must necessarily be barren of gold. The principal gold veins may geologically be classified in the following manner:—

Rocks.		
Metamorphic,	...	Nevada, Siberia, India.
Archæan,	...	Canada, Brazil, West Africa.
Cambrian,	...	Nova Scotia, Brazil.
Silurian,	...	Victoria, Otago (New Zealand), French Guiana.
Devonian,	...	Siberia, New South Wales.
Carboniferous,	...	Gympie (Queensland).
Jurassic,	...	Mexico.
Triassic,	...	California, Mexico.
Cretaceous,	...	Dakota, Hungary.
Tertiary,	...	United States, Australia.
Eruptive,	...	Hungary, Ural, India, Australia, Siberia, Borneo, Hauraki (New Zealand), Murchison (Western Australia).

Hennen Jennings' presidential address to the Institution of Mining and Metallurgy. London, March, 1903.

This is the latest resume of the modern position of Gold Mining and Metallurgy, and a practical exposition of main factors in the Cost of production.

TABLE I.—SELECTED MINES.—COSTS 1882-86.   *Hamilton Smith.*

MINE.	Period.	No. of Stamps.	Tons Crushed per year.	Tons per Stamp per Month.	Costs Milling per ton. Shillings.	Costs, Total, per ton. Shillings.
Sierra Buttes, - -	1885	76.5	54,493	59	2·33	24·25
Plumas Eureka, -	1885	60	55,973	78	2·54	23·17
Homestake, - -	1882-3	200	170,074	75	4·87	16·76
,,	1883-4	200	191,505	80	5·03	17·43
,,	1884-5	200	213,190	89	4·20	13·52
Father De Smet, -	1883	100	104,100	85	——	10·30
,,	1885	100	106,855	89	——	8·82
Caledonia, - -	1885 6	—	48,848	—	3·66	12·27
El Callao, - -	1882	60	22,405	31	46·55	188·61
,,	1883	60	24,750	34	——	184·41
,,	1884	60	30,936	43	30·16	146·31
,,	1885	80	47,223	49	20·72	91·35
,, (New Mill),	May, 1886	40	——	83	12·50	62·50
New Potosi, - -	11 Mos. 1884.	25.5	7,456	27		195·35

TABLE III.—RAND COMPANIES.—COSTS AND RESULTS.

DESCRIPTION OF MINES.	No. of Stamps.	*Tons Milled.	Yield per ton Milled.	Tons Cyanided (and Concentrates).	Yield by Cyanide (and Concentrates) on basis of per ton Milled.	Total Recovery
			s. d.		s. d.	s. d.
A. Mines that have paid a dividend during period under review. - - 18 Companies,	1,625	2,489,900	29 10	1,695,600	12 7	42 5
B. Mines that have made a profit, but have not paid a dividend during period, 7 do.	561	666,300	25 8	449,900	11 0	36 8
C. Mines that have made a loss during the period, - - - - 4 do.	270	288,300	19 11	280,600	10 5	30 4
	2,456	3,444,500	28 3	2,426,100	12 1	40 5

*The ore mined exceeded the ore milled by 300,000 tons owing to the sorting out of poor ore.

TABLE II.—ALASKA TREADWELL MINE.   COSTS IN 1896.

263,670 tons per year milled	
Mining. - -	2·29 Shillings per ton.
Milling. - -	1·45
Chlorination, - -	·47
General Expenses, -	·43
London Expenses, -	·05
Bullion Charges. &c., -	·15
Total Operating Costs,	4·85
Nett Profit, -	7·86
Total yield, -	12·71 Shillings per ton.

TABLES.

The three Tables of Costs shewn on these pages are condensed from Mr. Hennen Jennings' Evidence on the subject before the Industrial Commission of Enquiry by the late Government of the South African Republic, 1897.

They are referred to in that book on the following pages :—

Analysis of Results of 29 Companies on the Rand during period covered by their last annual Reports.

WORKING COSTS ON BASIS OF PER TON MILLED.									Profit per Ton.	Loss per Ton.
Mining.	Development Redemption.	Transport.	Total Mining Development Transport.	Milling.	Cyaniding and Concentrates.	General Charges.	Depreciation.	Total.		
s. d.	s. d.	s. d.	s. d.	s. d.	s. d.	s. d.	s. d.	s. d.	s. d.	s. d.
12 10	3 10	0 1·5	16 10	3 7	3 1	2 7	3 6	29 7	13 4	
14 4	4 6	0 1·6	18 11	3 8	2 10	2 7	4 10	32 10	3 9	
15 0	7 6	0 1·8	22 8	4 4	4 9	4 7	2 8	39 0		8 6
13 4	4 3	0 1·5	17 9	3 8	3 2	2 9	3 8	31 0		

WORLD'S PRODUCTION OF GOLD—

From the time of discovery of America till the end of 1900.

The following table by Dr. Adolph Soetbeer is taken from the Mineral Industry, vol. III, page 299, but herein the Kilogrammes have been calculated into Troy ounces.

	Ounces of Fine Gold.
1493-1600,	24,252,000
1601-1700,	29,330,000
1701-1800,	61,088,000
1801-1900,	357,692,000

The Century of 1801-1900 is shewn by decades in the following :—

	Ounces of Fine Gold.
1801-1810,	5,716,000
1811-1820,	3,680,000
1821-1830,	4,570,000
1831-1840,	6,523,000
1841-1850,	17,605,000
1851-1860,	59,992,000
1861-1870,	53,681,000
1871-1880,	50,450,000
1881-1890,	51,964,000
1891-1900,	103,521,000

The World's Production for 1899-1902 is set out in detail. (See Page 205.)

WORLD'S PRODUCTION OF GOLD—

By the Cyanide Process, from its introduction till the end of 1900.

The following figures are obtained principally from a paper read by Mr. G. T. Beilby to the Society of Chemical Industry, and published in their Journal of 28th February, 1898, supplemented by later information supplied by the Cassel Gold Extracting Company, Limited, Glasgow.

	Transvaal.	United States of America.	New Zealand.	Mexico.	Australia.	India.	Total.
1891	35,000	......	......	......	......	......	35,000
1892	175,000	......	......	......	......	......	175,000
1893	330,000	......	38,160	......	......	......	368,160
1894	600,000	......	86,728	......	......	158	686,886
1895	655,000	75,000	68,354	4,053	......	3,177	805,584
1896	770,000	135,700	119,091	9,931	......	5,364	1,040,086
1897	825,000	190,000	263,076	10,207	308,000	18,798	1,615,081
1898	......	245,840	422,418	61,460	398,074	30,440	1,158,232
1899	......	428,400	496,900	61,000	545,563	35,776	1,567,639
1900	......	487,280	452,524	60,000	683,899	59,414	1,743,117
Ounces of Bullion.	**3,390,000**	**1,562,220**	**1,947,251**	**206,651**	**1,935,536**	**153,127**	**9,194,785**

The above figures give the production of Bullion, and not of Fine Gold. The value of Bullion varies very much in different districts, being sometimes as low as 20 shillings per ounce in New Zealand and Queensland. Mr. Beilby states in his paper that the figures he gives for New Zealand may be taken at 20 shillings per ounce, which is rather under 250 fine—that is to say, in each ounce of Bullion there are only $\frac{242}{1000}$ parts of Fine Gold—but as an average over the whole world he assumes a figure of 750 fine. A large part of the balance of the Bullion is often Silver.

There was production of gold by the Cyanide Process in Australia earlier than 1897 though the figures are not obtainable.

WORLD'S PRODUCTION OF GOLD—for the last four years.

The Tables are from the most recent volumes of "Mineral Industry."

EUROPE.	1899.	1900.	1901.	1902.
Austria, ...	2,434	2,279	1,498	1,498
Hungary, ...	98,677	105,143	105,931	105,931
France, ...	8,681	6,527	Nil.	Nil.
Germany, ...	3,601	3,601	2,894	2,894
Italy, ...	3,643	1,849	132	132
Norway, ...	74	87	129	129
Russia, ...	1,159,214	1,072,434	1,253,592	1,183,379
Spain and Portugal,	394	461	579	579
Sweden, ...	3,414	3,414	2,016	2,016
Turkey, ...	375	375	1,479	1,479
United Kingdom, ...	2,845	12,760	5,189	5,189
	1,283,352	1,208,930	1,373,439	1,303,226
ASIA.				
Borneo (British), ...	11,168	19,873	12,095	12,095
China, ...	273,246	208,031	145,138	193,517
East Indies (Dutch),	7,234	26,609	27,425	31,800
India (British), ...	457,021	512,710	455,870	468,495
Japan, ...	53,998	68,485	79,729	79,729
Korea, ...	70,954	87,882	111,272	217,706
Malay Peninsula, ...	16,459	17,048	18,338	18,338
	890,080	940,638	849,867	1,021,680
AFRICA.				
Transvaal, ...	3,529,826	348,760	238,991	1,704,410
Abyssinia, ...	20,126	33,865	33,865	33,865
Rhodesia, ...	54,241	79,354	148,753	172,899
Soudan, ...	2,701	2,701	2,701	2,701
West Coast, ...	33,978	36,284	30,000	19,352
Madagascar, ...	11,060	33,471	26,332	26,332
Mozambique, ...	5,416	8,475	12,377	7,257
	3,657,348	542,910	493,019	1,966,816
AMERICA, NORTH.				
United States, ...	3,391,196	3,781,310	3,805,500	3,870,000
Canada and Newfoundland,	1,021,971	1,352,576	1,185,575	1,007,447
Mexico, ...	448,832	455,204	499,725	546,373
Central America, ...	25,402	38,703	42,332	45,960
	4,886,401	5,627,793	5,533,132	5,469,780
AMERICA, SOUTH.				
Argentina, ...	3,628	2,112	2,112	2,900
Bolivia, ...	7,256	7,257	7,257	7,257
Brazil, ...	107,644	127,820	133,636	146,898
Chili, ...	46,110	43,541	21,771	24,189
Colombia, ...	111,272	111,272	100,145	101,597
Ecuador, ...	6,047	9,676	12,700	13,304
Guiana (British), ...	108,269	110,640	92,032	88,492
Guiana (Dutch), ...	26,972	27,082	24,203	18,892
Guiana (French), ...	80,072	68,353	101,340	115,744
Peru, ...	41,635	52,480	80,369	82,245
Uruguay, ...	1,961	2,283	1,587	1,608
Venezuela, ...	49,191	49,194	38,704	38,704
	590,058	611,710	615,856	641,830
AUSTRALASIA, ...	3,810,130	3,568,279	3,719,103	3,989,083
Unspecified ...	21,771	21,771	21,771	21,771
Ounces of Fine Gold,	**15,139,140**	**12,522,031**	**12,606,187**	**14,414,186**

SOME NOTES

ON

ORGANIZATION FOR THE HEAD OFFICE.

When the Head Office of a Mining Company is at a distance from the Mine a separate Staff and Organization becomes necessary.

If the Company be not a large one, it may be convenient that its business be transacted in an office the expenses of which it shares with other Companies—either by paying a fixed annual sum for the use of office and secretarial and clerical services, or on the co-operative system of an assessment of the expenses *pro rata*.

Having set out how the books at the Mine are made up, it only remains to sketch very briefly an organization at the Head Office for taking these in hand and throwing the figures obtained into a convenient shape, such as is shewn on pages 201 and 202 in dealing with the results of the Witwatersrand Mines.

The following are some of the more important features of such an organization :—

Members of the Board of Directors.—One or more should be practical mining men, accustomed to take the lead in managing mining business, and conversant with all its details.

Technical Adviser.—There should be a Consulting Mining Engineer appointed by the Board to check estimates, prepare specifications and plans, and tabulate the returns of the mining and milling operations furnished by the manager, and advise as to machinery required or asked for by the manager at the Mine, as well as advise generally upon technical matters as they arise. Other technical advice by specialists in Metallurgical, Electrical or Mechanical matters may be obtained from time to time as occasion arises.

Secretary of the Company.—This officer should be a duly qualified man of business, who has had a large experience of Mining affairs, acquired on the best lines and under the best training.

He should be well acquainted with all matters connected with the transfer and registration of stocks and shares, and with the regulations of the Companies Acts.

He should also have a good knowledge of Mining Accounts, and be able, if necessary, to establish the accounts on a proper system, both at the Head Office and at the Mine.

He ought to examine the Forms and Returns received from the Mine as described in the foregoing pages, and see that the information required is being regularly supplied.

Internal or Directors' Auditors.—Where the operations are extensive the Board may find it useful to employ an auditor (other than the auditor appointed at the General Meeting) to supervise the mine accounts as they come to hand from month to month, so as to see that they are rendered in a proper and systematic manner. Such continuous audit might prevent in many cases unnecessary expenditure at the mines, or discrepancies and irregularities at the Head Office, which otherwise might not be noticed till the Annual Balance of the Company's accounts.

Registers.—Separate registers should be kept of Letters, Cables, Plans, Samples, and of Assay Results, in the same form as kept at the Mine, and shewn on pages 22, 23, and 27.

Letters and Cablegrams.—Copies of all letters and cablegrams sent to and received from the Mine should be sent to each Director immediately on their despatch or receipt. This saves time at the Board meetings, and enables the individual directors to follow more intelligently the course of operations at the Mine than if the correspondence were hurriedly read at these meetings. Letters received from the mine should be put on a special file, and the subjects carefully indexed; the outward letters should also be indexed.

Correspondence controlled by the Directors.—Communications to the Mine should in every instance be authorized by one or two of the Mining Directors before being sent off.

Budget.—Before any extension of plant, of development, or other special work is undertaken, a complete estimate of its cost should be prepared and submitted to the Board for approval. It will be found of use also to obtain monthly from the Mine an estimate of the monthly cash requirements for several months ahead under the usual departmental headings. In like manner estimates of costs in mining and reduction of ore should be made, and the monthly costs compiled from Form No. 8 should be carefully compared with the estimates.

Cash in Hand and Investments.—A statement of cash in hand, Bank Pass Book, certificate of the bank balance, and list of securities should be produced at each Board meeting, and the securities themselves at intervals.

Stores.—It would be found useful to obtain from the Mines office a monthly statement of the stocks in hand of the principal stores used, and how long they are expected to last. Such a statement enables it to be seen at a glance whether there is any excess stock of any one item.

Liabilities.—All accounts should be entered as soon as received in a book kept for the purpose, and placed before the Board at each meeting.

Tenders for Machinery and Stores.—For all descriptions of Machinery and Stores required, tenders should be invited. These should be considered by a Committee of the Board, and recommendations made as to their acceptance.

Expenditure at the Mine.—The total of the costs at the Mine should be received by cable monthly, whether the Mine is in the developing or producing stage.

Examination of Departmental Reports and Account Books.—The Reports and Accounts received from the Mine according to the system of Organization of Mining business set out in the foregoing pages, should be filed away in some convenient form, such as in special Guard Books, and the items from the Cash Book, Purchase Day Book, Sales Day Book, and Journal, posted monthly to a separate Ledger, which becomes a duplicate of the one kept at the mine. Some Companies journalize the monthly returns from the mine into accounts opened in the London Ledger, but it has been found more convenient to have a separate Ledger for the Mines accounts. The closing entries at the end of the year, coming through the Mines Journal, are posted in the ordinary way to the duplicate of the Mines Ledger and the corresponding entries are then made in the London books. The Mines account in the London Ledger should agree with the London office account in the Mines Ledger.

The monthly statements from the mine should be carefully examined and the Wages and Stores Sheets and Summaries compared with the General Expenditure Sheet.

At the end of the financial year and after the audit has been completed it is recommended that all the papers and returns in connection with the year's accounts be bound in one book in a convenient form for reference. Such book could be titled "Mines Returns, Inventories, and Accounts, and Head Office Statements for the year ending................."

Mining, Milling, Development, Power, Erection and other Departmental Reports, should at the end of the year be bound in a similar manner to the Accounts.

Visit to the Mine of Directors or Technical Adviser.—At least once a year there should be a visit paid by one or other of the aforesaid to the mine.

Model of the Mine.—It is strongly recommended that, in addition to the usual Mining Plans, Progress Sections, Assay Plans, and similar detail plans sent to the Head Office from the Mine, a model of the Mine should be constructed from such plans for the purpose of keeping the progress of work and development of the Mine constantly before the Board.

Staff.—Clerks to assist in dealing with any of the technical part of the work should be specially selected for this purpose.

The Secretary and his clerks should not be allowed to deal speculatively directly or indirectly in the shares of the Company.

Agents of the Company Abroad.—It is often desirable to have a reliable Agent or Agents in the neighbourhood of the Company's Mine, who could carry out the wishes of the Directors, and acting independently of the Manager, report to them all that was going on from time to time, as well as give the Manager the benefit of his advice as to Local and Mining Laws in force, and assist him with his general knowledge of the district.

All the Officials serving the Company should be chosen according to their ascertained qualifications for the several branches of the business, either technical or commercial.

The testimonials of officials should be rigidly enquired into by the Board, and copies filed for eventual reference in case of need.

" 𝔚e rather shew the way to the ignorant
than prescribe order to the learned."—
𝔉rom 𝔄ncient 𝔅ook of 𝔒rder.

INDEX.

CPSIA information can be obtained at www.ICGtesting.com
Printed in the USA
BVOW09s1001230315

392874BV00016B/239/P